Dedicated to my parents:
Constant Georges MERITZA
(1929-2011)
Josiane MERITZA
(1936-)
and the woman who shares my life
my partner Sophie

Special dedication:

Yoann MERITZA

HOW TO REPROGRAM YOUR SUBCONSCIOUS MIND?

Editorial:
BoD-Books on Demand,
12/14 rond point des Champs Élysées
75008 Paris, France
Printing: BoD-Books on Demand, Norders-
tedt, Allemagne
legal deposit September 2018
ISBN: 9782322152063
Cover photo :
License: universal cco 1.0 / (cco 1.0)
Graphic design: Yoann MERITZA
from the book in french:
"Comment reprogrammer son subconscient?"
Copyright 00064891-1- © Yoann MERITZA
September 2018 - rights reserved

"Between what I think, what I want to say, what I think I say, what I say, what you want to hear, what you hear, what you think you understand, what you want to understand and what you understand, there are at least ten possibilities (but in reflection for the tenth ...) of not understanding, but let's try it anyway. "
("New Encyclopedia of Relative and Absolute Knowledge" Bernard Werber)

SOME WORDS ABOUT THE AUTHOR

Yoann MERITZA is an essayist author passionate about personal development and human behavior.

Born on March 28, 1978 in Bonneville, Haute-Savoie in a working class family. He've benefited of schooling in private Catholic institutions, particularly in *Sainte Bernadette* and *Saint Jean Bosc*o in Cluses, in his birth department.

His father, Constant Georges, who died on July 5, 2011 at the age of 81, a veteran of Indochina, a former member of the TOE-GCI, a civilian truck driver, suffered from throat cancer in 1981, always fought and cultivated enthusiasm to despite her disability, because he understood how precious life was and that he had to live it intensely. He was a veteran during both the Indochina war, and fought for the rest of his life.

Yoann was immersed in this environment in which he had to fight every day, he always tried to keep going no matter what happened and tried new experiences.

He followed normal schooling until 1993 before going to an apprenticeship school in Saint Jeoire where he discovered the trades of electrician, carpenter, bar tilter and welder, which made him a "*chopper of all trades*".

In September 1995, a new turning point in his life, he followed a career in the tertiary accounting sector at the *Lycée Professionnel Privé "les cordeliers"* in Cluses, where he discovered office automation and administration, and also learned about the technologies of the information for management, which he continues to use today in his private life. But he lost his BEP for a few points.

Under the direction of his former accounting professor, he repeated his BEP in 1998, which he obtained.

From February 1999 to December of the same year, he performed his national service in Auxonne in Burgundy in the *511th Regiment of the train*, then in the *27th BCA* in Cran-Gevrier in Haute-Savoie.

After leaving the army, he decided to try his bachelor's degree in accounting as a free candidate, worked for months in all subjects, became his "*own teacher*", even today, self-taught to the core, he knew how to "*train him-*

self", obtained his diploma, but he decided not to stop, feeling that he was growing wings, he worked in the industry to finance his studies by correspondence, which was for him "*a great piece*", every night after his classes, but the results were scarce for him .

He undertook to resume studies in a recurrent session in 2001, at the request of the training centers and the "*Center for Information and Guidance*" (COI), where he was followed by a counselor who helped him fill in the necessary forms for his reintegration into the professional cycle.

In September 2001, he returned to the *Lycée Guillaume Fiche*t, was then 23 years old, four of which separated him from the other students, a slight generational shock that he managed to compensate, he adapted very well to this environment, and in June 2003 he obtained his professional baccalaureate in accounting.

He tried by all means to pass his BTS, because by age 25 he was too old for employers, when it came to immersing himself in a professional environment in two years. He suffered defeats, but he did not admit defeat. He attended some seminars for the main automobile brands, especially in Valence, in the Drôme region.

In 2004, he took advantage of a golden opportunity following a training as a SME / SMI collaborator at the *Chamber of Commerce and Industry* of Scionzier in Haute-Savoie, where he discovered NLP (Neuro-Linguistic Programming) where he learned the tools to mold the subconscious mind and direct human nature

From 2007 until now, he has been interested in the topics of personal development, subconscious control and has read many books on topics of psychology and behavior, he has also attended coaching seminars. It still follows, and fairly regularly, personal development coaches.

He is also a member of the *National Union of Combatants* (UNC-Alpes), and of the *27th BCA*.

FOREWORD

Hello to all my readers friends!

Finally here we are, a new book on personal development, took time, but finally we arrived, which means that with a little will, we can do everything, I show it again.

After my first book "*Guaranteed Success*", I came up with the idea of a second book, without really knowing what I was going to talk about and where to start.

For the occasion, I was going to do something very special, what else could I do that does not currently exist and could help many people around the world?

So I had the idea of making my own book dedicated to the subconscious mind. There are already some, I know, but very few are suitable for any audience, I had to do something compatible with all levels of knowledge.

Many people will find that my approaches are simplistic, I would respond that it is voluntary. What is available to some is not available to everyone, I think it is "collective", that is, at any sociocultural level, there is no need for prerequisites, everyone can assimilate the lines of this book without too many difficulties .

I had to gather a lot of information on the subject to write it, and in summary, it is partly what I will talk about, the search for new information.

Most of you have already tried to learn about the subject through the Internet, and I know how frustrating it is to be in places that offer evasive or complicated answers, the authors of these pages do not reach everyone and do not realize that This same public does not assimilate everything easily.

What makes this book unique is both a personal interpretation of the laws of the subconscious mind, the result of extensive research with specialists in the field, including reading the works of *Dr. Joseph Murphy*, as well as providing a new perspective in our way of thinking, to create something for the use of all without distinction, limiting or even banishing all scientific expressions.

It is a practical book that everyone can get, and my willingness to write it is to help as many people as possible by keeping everyone up-to-date.

I will summarize the main lines of this book to facilitate understanding, which has been divided into two main parts, one theoretical and one practical.

Our brain is a huge database where billions of data are transmitted every second to allow our body to operate and store the data we receive throughout our lives from birth.

In this same brain, three functions share the place, there is first the consciousness that interacts with our external world, the unconscious where the imaginary and creative spirit that constitutes our inner world resides, and the subconscious, the great decision-maker of our actions and interpretations towards the external world, in direct relation with our experience.

The latter validates or not (without us really wanting) what we think or imagine, is the referee of everything we recorded in memory.

There are two very important phases in the thought process, what we know and what we think we know, what has been learned incorrectly, either by a third person or interpreted according to what we have experienced (and not necessarily what we know)), and what is real (knowledge).

There are specific criteria for our own thoughts, they come from what we have learned from our family, friends, teachers, as well as from our own experiences, for example, as a child, if you have burned yourself with a radiator, the information that will result in your subconscious It is pain, and throughout your life you will be careful with the radiators.

If you are a victim of phobias such as fear of spiders, closed places, cats or any other form of fear, correspond to what I just said.

In short, all that shapes our subconscious is an accumulation of direct interactions with the outside world, but also, the creations of our inner world (the unconscious).

So, we have a first question, if a brain can be programmed, is it possible to reprogram it? Of course, all you have to do is reinterpret our old thoughts and beliefs of our subconscious, our memory is part of us, unless there is a general amnesia, which does not mean to erase all our experience, but to interrupt the connections neuro-associated.

On the other hand, it is possible to modify the access roads to our subconscious mind, create new connections that allow you to validate new information, in this book, I will show you how to proceed, and with some examples.

For this, in the first part, I will talk about this wonderful machine that allows us to think and act. You will discover how information flows, why you think in this way and how it is possible to question the way you think or act.

You will also discover the wonderful power of creativity and imagination, how the great pioneers created our daily life, what allows us to drive a car, have light, have fun, all this comes from your subconscious, the great information bank that provided the necessary elements for the unconscious (the imaginary).

For example, if you like to make crafts and want to build a cabin (in your imagination), you will need wood, tools and nails, so you get them in the DIY store (the subconscious) that will provide everything you need to do it.

In the second part of this book, you will learn to reprogram your subconscious mind (since that is what it is about), and to become a better version of yourself. But it will require a personal investment, and my role is to provide you with all the tools and techniques necessary to achieve it. Everything else depends on your willingness to act, and in this, even providing you with the right tools, your personal investment is yours.

You will also learn why you surrender so close to the goal, to not want or to postpone, you will expel those bad habits that poison your life, you will adopt a new lifestyle, success will become your reason for being.

My goal is to help you regain maximum control of your destiny, you will have to banish many of your old beliefs and adopt new ones, and you will see that it will be better.

To conclude, without a doubt, all the methods in this book can only work, because they really are, I invite you to take control and do not believe all those who sell you dreams and imagination, the real power is only in you.

We hope this book will provide you with everything you need.

Friendly yours

Yoann MERITZA

INTRODUCTION

«A library is the crossroads of the dreams of all humanity. »
(Julien Green)

Today is a great day, the opening of a new library in the city. The residents were delighted with the event, and everyone brought something for its opening. One of the "*Sophie*" (because it is a very common name in this community) had brought sandwiches and soda cans. With the mini-market closed, he had used a vending machine at a gas station to get his supplies, making the company responsible for supplying these machines happy, and the ire of the truckers who wanted to take a small sandwich.

Many personalities such as *Bernard Henry Levy* were even invited, he could not free himself when he was very busy, in his place was *Bertrand Pinot*, specialized in wine guides and resident in a nearby town, his speech could be limited to the national vineyards.

The mayor of the city did not take his suit to the dry cleaner, because it was closed like any other store (including the minibar), by decision of the member of the highest headquarters of the municipality, who had the "*Brilliant idea*" to make the day of the inauguration a day of rest for the inhabitants of the city.

Failing that, he took what he had at hand, his suit, which dates back ten years and which, apparently, is narrow and smells like naphthalene.

The night goes well, fireworks, dances, music with the hearts of the *Priory of Santa Cecilia*, who arrived with great reinforcement of the Luberon in truck, their vehicle had been broken, *Ed Sheera*n couldn't to come to at the invitation. He could'nt to be liberated (decisively) At the same time, he gave a concert in Seattle, and why settle in this small city of France, inhabited by only thirty people?

The speech was short because there was not much to say, *Bertrand Pinot* was only here to promote the vineyards of his wine guide, and the mayor having left his speech in the pocket of his suit (the dry cleaner), his speech was brief   .

But what about this great library? The architect intervened at night to praise them, leaving a variety of books, or rather, a variety of places to place them.

Why does it say that? Because it is desperately empty, what is the meaning of building of that? This afternoon was a succession of fatal disappointments, *Bertrand Pinot*, *the priory of Sainte Cécile*, the mayor in his suit that shows his robustness and the absence of his speech perfumed with dry cleaning solvent, and the little Sophie with his sandwiches that can be found in the vending machines on the road.

You will probably wonder what is the use if there is nothing to read, that is the question that the people of this city have also asked themselves. As a result, a person responsible for the project to create this library, seeing that desperately empty shelves had a brilliant idea (the first of all), summoned all the inhabitants to a meeting.

During his speech, he asked the inhabitants to give all the books they no longer read, and to come and put them in the library on the shelves, *Bertrand Pinot* was the first, we can imagine it.

Thus, the people of this city returned to their respective homes, each emptying their attics of old and dusty books that they no longer needed, and taking them back to the library. But this one has two great alleys, one called "*para-dise*" and the other "*hell*". At the bottom of these are the files. The books were left in dis-array.

Those responsible for the project named a li-brarian who hastened to put all these works in order, the task was dangerous and long, not all of us call ourselves *Bertrand Pinot*, because it is he who was chosen for lack of staf, there was more than thirty thousand of books on the shelves, and there was also space available to accommodate new ones.

The visitors, many of whom helped fill the shelves, got lost, the categories did not match what they were looking for, children's litera-ture was in the science fiction section, adven-ture stories on the shelves for romance, they lost time finding their way in the corridors. We wonder if Bertrand Pinot don't make onlyone to writing wine guides.

The librarian was replaced, and each book found its desired place (according to the new person named for the position), but despite this, most visitors did feel bothered by these changes.

This great library is you, or at least your brain, guides the vehicle that allows you to evolve in this world and interact with the outside world, that is, with your body.

The shelves are your memory, from birth they are empty and filled from the first moments of your life.

The books symbolize their knowledge, depending on whether they are stored in paradise or in the hall of hell.

The files represent your subconscious mind, it is the place where all the memories are stored. (previous knowledge)

The inhabitants are the interactions with your environment, the people you know in your life come to deposit the books that represent the information (later knowledge).

And finally, the one that has the worst role is the conscience, in the form of a librarian, classifies the given books (interactions) in the two corridors of the shelves, one represents your good choices (heaven), and the other, your bad decisions (hell). It refers to the files (subconscious) to store them. Sometimes the little librarian does what he wants.

As for me, I am here to put order in the archives, to help you make the right decisions, so that you return to the right path. My task is not simple, I will have to readjust your subconscious mind that will not necessarily assimilate everything that I will give you, convince a librarian who stands firm in his positions, but with your help, we will fight him.

To do this, first I will show you the plans of this great library, I will put the knowledge books on the correct shelves and corridors, and I will also add new ones.

Let's go immediately at the discovery of your brain and put it in order!

PART 1: DISCOVERING OUR SUBCONSCIOUS

CHAPTER 1: HOW DOES IT WORK?

"There may not be a day in our childhood
that we lived as fully as we thought we had
left without living them, the ones we had with
a favorite book."
(Marcel Proust)

Understanding our subconscious mind

We will get to the heart of the matter and try to
give a fairly precise definition of the subconscious mind, who is it and what is it for? Many
confuse conscious, unconscious and subconscious, to help you understand their functions,
let me show you their difference.

First, there is the consciousness that works in
interaction with the outside world, in connection with a direct reflection related to our habits of daily life and your memories, is the
mind awake, when you take a drink, when you
read, play sports or another activity, you do it
in full consciousness and with a little reflection, you think about it and act accordingly.
Act in accordance with your five senses, and
the subconscious mind is the referee. When
you are focused, it means that nothing else interacts between what you are experiencing outside of yourself, and the recording of data in

the subconscious, during a conversation, you listen to the instructions of your boss, the interaction is direct, you are not distracted by other elements external, the mind focuses on what he says.

As for the unconscious, it is the sleeping mind, it is the seat of our imagination and dreams, it is our world and it communicates with the subconscious mind from which it originates to create something new that it will then store in the great memory bank. Great artists focus on the inner world from what they already know and transcribe it, through the subconscious mind, into the real world. Sometimes it makes us commit acts whose value judgments are reinterpreted by the subconscious, in this case, the conscience is based only on the interactions with the inner world, it has often been said "*but, what an unconscious!*" Is because in these specific cases, you were not paying attention. It acts according to its own inner world, the outer world is reinterpreted. This happens when, for example, you are in the middle of a job and you think about many things inside of you, so you are no longer focused on what you are doing, or at least partially.

And then there is the subconscious, this is the subject that we will discuss in this book, it interacts with your conscious and unconscious, both the inner and outer world. It is the home of our oldest archived memories and operates on the basis of a value judgment. Your feelings in connection with the stages of your life are written in it, act not only with words, but also with emotions related to consciousness and the creations of the unconscious. The subconscious mind is in a way the referee of our thoughts.

The origin of our old information

From the first day of your life, your parents offered a book to your subconscious called "paradigm", its classification on the shelves of this great library of which I spoke in the introduction will have a decisive impact on the rest of your life. In this book we find the primary information, which molds our minds, is at the heart of what makes us evolve in this world from our birth and our first steps in life.

The librarian (conscience), curious about everything, will read it in secret and classify it according to his feelings in *"heaven"* or *"hell"*, far away, where the two rows are located near the archives. Consciousness can write new chapters of our lives within this great library, an intelligent combination of old information, stored in a new way called "*unconscious*" or "*imaginary*". This point of origin will create connections with another book called "*Childhood*", which contains all the chapters of your youth, both good and bad moments.

From then on, new books will complete the collection, both those you receive and those you believe, the farther you go in life, and the more new books you add, the corridors complement each other and take you away from the first book whose location alone the librarian (your conscience) knows, unless he has gaps in his memory. Our first steps in life are decisive, are those that shape the rest of our existence, making us follow a path, then another, and one thing leads to the other, takes us to the page you read for example, that is, to the point where you are now.

This does not mean that everything is lost, and yes! You have my book that you can add to your own collection in your bookshelves, however, it will not do everything, it will only give you clues to follow, but what is really happening in your head (your value judgments) depends on you, I will I will show the way, but it is up to you to follow it.

If in your youth you have been banned, intimidated or discouraged, this information will be stored by your subconscious mind and the emotions associated with it, and it is your subconscious mind that decides what behavior to adopt based on what it has collected. How to classify the information, in "*pain*" or "*pleasure*", in "*paradise*" or "*hell*".

Although as an adult (I do not know exactly where you are in relation to your age), if you have forgotten or want to forget, there are still in your subconscious the references to painful or joyful episodes recorded inside you. In the yard of the school or in the family, you heard unpleasant things about yourself, that you were incapable, that you were good for nothing, null, your malleable mind accepted the information, and this triggered a blocking mechanism. This not only makes your memories speak, but also associates them with a relative feeling.

This blockage is caused by the sociocultural barrier that does not invite you to go beyond your possibilities.

In fact, your perception of the outside world is shaped by all the beliefs that have been inculcated in you and your interpretation of the environment that surrounds you.

In a nutshell, imagine a border post run by an alcoholic customs officer, *Sergeant Pastaga* (my mind whispers it to me, I do not know why).

He tells you anything under the influence of drunkenness, that it is impossible for you to cross the barrier, because you are not part of the initiates, the new world is not for you, and you are restricted to remain in the old, that is, in your current life.

On the other side of that border is the life you want to have, you look at it from afar, but you do not run the risk of irritating the customs officer under the influence of alcohol, because you do not know how to force the way and break that barrier, you will have to establish a plan of action, and for that, you will need new information in the form of books, it is not your entourage that will help you, otherwise, you would have crossed the border since a long time ago, but stay with you, for fear of facing anger of the customs officer who is restless in the distance.

The knowledge will be your passport or the way to break this barrier, you know how to use it, because the new world is full of educated people, you will not be accepted there and if you want to accelerate the events to get there, you can also take a truck and break the barrier by not hitting *Sergeant Pastaga*, who will sound the alarm, and in great reinforcement, will take you back across the border.

You can also obtain a passport and request information from the customs officer, who will give you the best. Bring him a good bottle of wine, that would make him happy. He will tell you that in order to obtain it, he has to go to a large administrative building called "*instruction*". In this building, there are several offices. In each of them, a document will be requested. The first one is called "*will*" and it is you who writes it!

Armed with this document, you go through a first office called "*English*", he puts his visa to go to the next room "*Mathematics*", then "*Science*", and so on until the last seal of the "*Trust*" seal.

Once the last stamp is applied, you can proudly imagine yourself facing *Sergeant Pastaga* with the precious document and a good bottle of *Gewurtstraminner*.

It will open the door to you in this new world

full of educated individuals who have done very well in their lives. The interaction will be between them, and you will not appear to be an imposter.

Going through the "*instruction*" offices was a long and dangerous journey, in phases of discouragement, but you kept the objective of going to the other side of the border, it will not have been easy, but you have achieved it.

The reference point

This is what is at the origin of your current thoughts from the first moments of your life. The first book of our entire existence entitled "*paradigm*" that creates the first neuro-associated connections about the information presented and the information withheld.

When we are born, our eyes open to the environment that will serve as the basis for our perception of everything that surrounds us. These perceptions are the foundations, it is from there that everything will be built, the first connections will be created with their memories, the memory is formed at the same time as their feelings related to it (conscious and subconscious connection). It is "*the point of refe-*

rence" (or origin), it is also the starting point of what we might call paradigms, a form of conscious mechanism that pushes us to act in one way or another, borrowing a certain pattern of behavior linked to a social group.

Depending on your background, you have learned to read, write, believe and prohibit, whether of ethnic, religious or cultural origin.

You are taught value systems, either for money or morals, notions of what is right and what is wrong, respect for others.

In our mind a seed was sown, watered with new information, which gave either a magnificent oak, or a weeping willow (to make a small analogy between strength and fragility).

To continue developing the principle of the tree, I recommend that you read *Max Piccinini's book "Success Max"* (no more word).

Neural connections

Our brain is formed by a tangle of intercommunicating networks, in which billions of pieces of information circulate every second and all have well-defined functions.

Some allow us to make our body work by pointing out our physiognomic needs, such as drinking, eating or sleeping, others allow us to move, walk, grasp objects, feel pain or pleasure. They are located in the cortex of the reptile (or primary brain), is the first layer of our brain and is what allows our organic structure to interact with the subconscious, when your body needs water to hydrate, sends a signal to the latter to indicate who is thirsty.

Then, the limbic cortex comes to cover it, stores all the information of our life, everything we have learned, the field of values is in this part. When you remember an event, it is him you call, it is also the seat of the subconscious mind. In this same cortex new information is recorded, and the combination of old and new data is made and interpreted (consciousness) or combined to create a new situation in your inner world (unconscious).

And finally, the neo cortex covers the limbic cortex, it is in this part that new information penetrates when the mind is awake, and it is also the place of external interactions. Our brain works through these three levels: the information enters, is treated and validated or not as a last resort. This is called thinking, a communication between incoming information and older information, or a communication between two existing elements in your subconscious, to create something new, called imagination.

If, for example, you watch a documentary about the Caribbean on television, you equate it with pleasure, and your emotions wake up, you have the desire to pack your bags and go on vacation, but you do not have the financial means to do so. The information enters and is processed by the subconscious mind that weighs the pros and cons, for what you already know, the state of your bank account, who will feed the cat, defend your case before the judge (your subconscious), the lawyers will declare, one is in favor (your unconscious), and formulates many strategies to achieve it, and the other against (your conscience), very realistic, is based only on reality, each one of them lists his version of the facts, but the judge gives his verdict, the trip impossible due to lack of financial means, the alleged is condemned to stay at home.

Of course, your subconscious mind is not only about giving good and bad points, but digging a little deeper will give you solutions to get there in the years to come. We went from "*I can not do it for ...*" to "*How can I do that?*" .

The unconscious will have time to prepare his statement. Connections are made, in relation to what we know and what we learn, it is like an addition that gives a result. Acting in the most complete ignorance, not resorting to their neuro-associated connections becomes unconscious, without thinking about your bank account, without thinking about your cat, leaving to the adventure as it is summarized in something unreflective, a fact that does not pass through awareness.

Sensorial connections

They are inscribed in the reptilian cortex, our five senses awaken in relation to them, what we see, what we touch, what we feel or hear gives new information to the subconscious. When we fall in love, our senses awaken in this part of the brain, if our eyes see a beautiful person in front of us that transmits information to our subconscious, this great center of memory processing, which associates it with pleasure. Respond with stimuli to our body, sweating, palpitations, etc ...

These connections allow us to appreciate or not the world around us, always referring to older information, associating the incoming data with pain or pleasure. But for this, if an individual does not know these sensations, such as heat or cold, when he discovers them, he will become the point of reference, for example, several years ago (long before the refrigerator was invented), many populations that they live in an equatorial climate they had no idea what the winter temperatures could be, their bodies were not used to it, but still they have this ability to adapt, sometimes giving the point of reference.

When transposing to the real world, let us suppose that the bank «Radin» calls you to review a loan file, the meaning used is to listen, the information is transmitted to the view that identifies the drawer that is to be opened, and then it is transmitted to the hand that makes the gesture of reaching the handle of that drawer (touch it). These three senses communicate with each other, the hand takes the sheet, touches it, gives the information to the view that identifies the document, and then reaches the vocal cords to transcribe what the view transmits.

What is also extraordinary is that these three senses follow more or less the same path that leads to the point of origin, the subconscious, the great center of information processing. He applics a value judgment to the information that our senses give him. Better yet, here I come to the meaning of my book, is that this storage center can be modified, create new connections and silence old ones. Take books from "*hell*" and put them in "*heaven*", and vice versa, although other works will remain in the dungeons.

The intercommunication of information

The information collected is intertwined with older information, giving them an interpretation, it works like this:

Here is a table coded by colors that shows the interpretations made by our brain.

Point of origin or old information	New identical information	Interpretations based on old and new information
Red	Yellow	Orange
Blue		Green

The first column represents the old information, what you have already learned, what your subconscious mind has already processed, is your point of origin, all the data already collected and interpreted.

The second represents new information, if the link is made with the point of origin, an interpretation of the information will be constructed from it. If it is still non-existent in your mind, it will be treated as it is, it is raw information, which does not exclude that these new data come from someone who has already made his own interpretation, it can be a writer or a philosopher who already has his own opinions and asks him to federate, in this very precise case, the void is filled with a basic data (or reference).

The third column is the result obtained between the two, we can translate it as a favorable or unfavorable opinion, and all this comes from your conscience.

The most revealing is talking to you about social conditioning, if you live in a modest environment, your opinions are directed towards socialism, otherwise, if you evolve in a rather liberal world, you will have opinions oriented towards capitalism, I assure you that this is a example mode, knowing that opinions are specific to each one.

For the socialists and capitalists, there is only one product of the "*UNTEL*" brand, one will say that this product is too expensive, the other will say that it is of good quality. Returning to our famous painting, we will replace the colors with the example I just gave.

Point of origin or old information (opinions)	New identical information	Interpretations based on old and new information
Socialist	Brand "UNTEL"	Too expensive
Capitalist		Quality product

For the same information given, two individuals will react differently according to their knowledge, experience and their social and cultural origin.

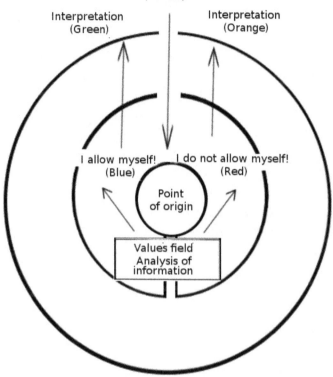

New information
(Yellow)

Interpretation
(Green)

Interpretation
(Orange)

I allow myself!
(Blue)

I do not allow myself!
(Red)

Point
of origin

Values field
Analysis of
information

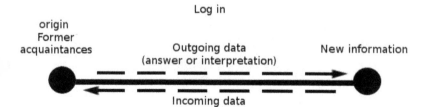

Log in

origin
Former
acquaintances

Outgoing data
(answer or interpretation)

New information

Incoming data

Know how to name things

The subconscious needs information to establish the connection between what we know or do not know and the object that is presented to us. Do you know that the Inuits know how to name the snow in different ways? Thanks to the knowledge that has been transmitted from generation to generation, but with respect to firearms, in the days of the pioneers of North America, they did not know its usefulness, because no cognitive connection was established between their ancestral knowledge. And firearms ended up giving meaning to that object, as well as a definition. "*Instrument that causes death*", anyway, a weapon (in a broad sense) is synonymous with death in most cases.

The ways of our brain

The information can follow three different access routes:

- from subconscious to conscious:
When it comes to calling your memory, for example, when someone asks you to remember a memory of your childhood, you respond directly by looking for information written in the subconscious mind.

- from subconscious to unconscious:
Old and new information creates something new by association, for example, if you imagine fire with the sensation of cold, of course, it does not exist in the real world, but sensory and visual stimuli are known to your subconscious. A blind person from his birth can only know the sensations of heat and cold, but he can imagine according to the information gathered by the ear of those around him. For a person who is blind in his life, the information continues to exist, a friend tells him "be careful with the fire in front of you", he will feel the heat and associate it with a mental image of flames.

- subconscious to conscious and unconscious:
Thanks to its ability to store neuro-associated combinations, this is what allows us to create from real information. The subconscious mind provides the unconscious with the old and new data provided by the conscience in order to imagine something new. When a person asks us a question about our lives, and we lie about our past, he goes through the same network.

To be more precise

Awareness
It is what allows us to interact with the outside

world, and gives the information to the sub-conscious mind that processes it according to ancient data. It is the seat of our thoughts.

The unconscious
It is what allows us to make neuroassociated combinations with old and new information, interacts with our inner world, is what gives us creative power when referring to the subconscious
.

The subconscious mind
It is a database where all the information collected by our inner and outer world is stored. It is here that all our memories are lodged, as well as the neuroasocitivities created by the conscious and the unconscious.

One thinks, the next stores and the third one imagines.

INFORMATION CIRCULATION

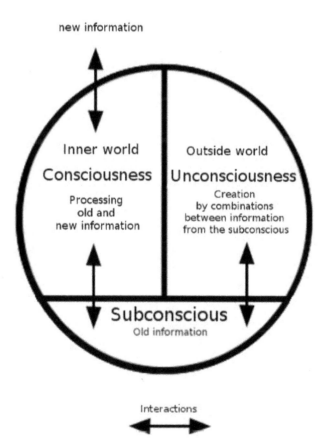

Neuro-associated Perceptions

If I say "*heavenly place*", what are you thinking about? And what does the term "*wealth*"
mean to you?

We all have different ways of thinking about
these terms, of feeling their impact on our
minds.

I'll give you some examples:

Jacques, who is Parisian, dreams of going on
vacation abroad, every day he goes to work,
on the way, he sees the Eiffel Tower, a monu-
ment he is used to seeing, is part of his daily
life. Even taking the air on the balcony. His
thoughts are not oriented towards this steel
building, he thinks about the West Indies, he
runs away from his mind and thinks about the
wonderful things he could do in those places,
he even has a poster hanging in his room. Palm
trees and a white sand beach.

In another part of the world, Simon, a young
West Indian who dreams of going to France, is
thinking about that. Where he lives, it is only
misery and everything that is proposed, are
small jobs, he thinks that all his problems will

be solved once there. In his room, he has a poster of the Eiffel Tower, for him, compared to his current life, it is a paradise, he imagines that he will earn a lot of money once there.

Perspective...

There is a notable difference between what we know and what we would like, we idealize images that are not real, Jacques considers his own hell in the form of Paris, with its subways, its stress, its traffic jams, are references that it has acquired during long time, on the other hand, Simon does not know this "Paris", for him, everything is beautiful and sweetened there. What seems to one person a hell, the other is not. Everyone has their own conception of hell or paradise, there is a limit between both, is the imagination.

We all dream of something better, but once we get it, we have the information we need to make our own judgment about values, to congratulate ourselves or to repent.

Another example: I have seen a report in a barracks about volunteers in the military for a long time. During one of the maneuvers, a group of young people consumed alcohol hidden in bottles, a wine residue used during an internal event in the barracks.

When the chiefs discovered this, all the young soldiers were invited to meet. They were ordered to present their bottle and empty it in front of them. Those who really had wine in it were severely punished and punished, because in the army it is considered a crime.

In this documentary, there was a scene in which a sergeant chief had taken one of the youths aside and had given him a sermon.

This scene has been repeated many times on social networks, in front of hilarious spectators. There have been parodies. Although the situation was funny, it was not for the Sergeant Major, who had the responsibility of supervising these young people, and the soldier, terrified, having understood his mistake, who let himself be indoctrinated by his group.

All this to tell you that there is a difference between what we see or hear, and what we experience or feel. In the case of the First Sergeant or the young man, how would some of the spectators have reacted? Would they die of fear like the soldier? Would they be annoying as the immediate superior? This shows that a single piece of missing information can disturb everything else, that an actor is not a spectator. There is no neuroassociative connection of pain with what you can see or hear, there is no feeling.

While I was still in training for my Professional Accounting Teaching Certificate, our class had to make a presentation. Excuse me if I do not remember the exact circumstances, but it was in relation to my title that I had to get. When it was my turn, I stood in front of the other students and I guarantee that there is nothing more stressful than an audience looking at you, what do you say at that moment? *"What will they think of my performance?"* I was sweating and stuttering, in short, a real disaster. I was focusing more on the judgments of others than on my own text that I had to read, so one of them finally answered (although not in the exact terms) "*it was pathe-*

tic!" It made me feel a little uncomfortable with the kind of response I gave him: "*Criticism is easy, art is difficult!*"

Shortly after, I left the room, disgusted with this type of behavior and disappointed with my own performance. While waiting for the results in another room, some students approached me and said: "*You should have listened to the one who said that your performance was not convincing, it did not work better*". (Out of respect for the other students of the time, no, I did not reveal a name),they showed me that not everyone thinks the same, those who came to join me were as disgusted as I was with his behavior.

All this to say that whoever found my disastrous performance was exactly in the same situation as me, moving from spectator to actor, so why did he do it? To drive the demons from their own fear over me? To do something interesting? I will probably never know!

The neuroassociated perception can take several aspects, by associating our knowledge with the outside world, providing new information, but also a new interpretation of the imaginary (the unconscious).

This is also what happens when someone creates a character. Take the example of an individual who has seen several war movies, from Rambo to Apocalypse Now, and has followed many documentaries about the army. He does not do it essentially for pleasure, even though it gives him pleasure, but he identifies with someone he is not. He idealizes himself by creating his own character, giving information to his subconscious, and the imagination makes associative neurological combinations through them. You will learn how an assault rifle works, all about the soldier's equipment, to create a memory, having a perception of the soldier as a brave person, who is not afraid, but lacks experience in the field. Certainly, he will know everything he needs to know, anyway, there are enough videos circulating on the subject, but when faced with reality, if a conflict breaks out, he will discover something he did not foresee in his "call" brave life, instinct of preservation.

There is a great void in the depths of itself that fills false information, this need to feel important in the eyes of others, is the fruit of the unconscious and not the subconscious, it is the imagination that dominates their minds, and the force of repetition, the risk is to end up suffocated by his own lie, imprisoned in a life he has not lived, which can lead to mental confusion and madness.

I have met people who have been involved in external conflicts, generally have good memories of them at the group level, but do not want to talk about them. Where is the merit when you take someone's life and risk yours? They want to forget what happened, some still have nightmares, there is something broken in them, and for others, the experience has hardened them, wanting to share their experience for preventive purposes.

I remember a soldier who volunteered when I was in national service in 1999, when there were still conflicts over the partition of the territory of Kosovo. He was a sergeant in charge and was part of the staff, but despite his rank, I can tell you that I saw him trembling, not knowing where he was going to land, on what terrain. His fear increased when he received his identification badges with his blood type, as well as the documents he had to sign regarding the people who should be informed in case of death. At the same time, he was worried about what was going to happen, he was completely disconnected from reality, his face had been bleached with fear, we tried to talk to him, he answered: "*Shut up! I'm concentrat-*

ing!" This sergeant was completely enclosed in himself, like a snail wrapped in a shell.

He had no idea what was going to happen, or how he was going to assume his role, a heavy responsibility fell on his shoulders.

Between imagining a war and doing it, there is a wide margin, and those who have returned from it are transformed forever, having to suspect day by day as if it were the last, afraid of receiving a stray bullet from a sniper. This is what happens in any conflict, the soldiers become mentally marked forever.

Generally, these people do not make any glory of it, not like this type of individuals who showed up one day at my brother's house, was a person from the neighborhood who said he had fought in the war, who saw it and experienced everything, it happened about ten years ago (around 2008), he wore a suit that made him look more like a vagabond than a poorly cared-for petty officer, and the insignias did not correspond in any way to what he said, because he had the ranks of cape major, while He claimed to be a lieutenant.

In our lives, we meet all sorts of people who lie ore create stories, but if we ourselves have already experienced this type of situation, it is easy to detect deception.

What we have to say to each other is that they are unhappy people who end up being absorbed by their lies and, above all, they end up alone.

I just hang out with real people and run away from others! Also, become this authentic person, along the path of knowledge and truth.

CHAPTER 2: THE LAWS OF THE SUB-CONSCIOUS MIND

"The laws of the universe are a simple construction of a part of the brain, while men and societies obey more their passions and prejudices. "
(Marc Gendron)

The subconscious mind is governed by five main laws, that of balance, knowledge, continuity, repetition and perseverance.

If you follow the principles that follow, you will get everything that life has to offer, you will have to draw from your inner strength, the one you find that keeps you going.

When I was younger, during my national service, I did maneuvers in Valdahon, during this period, my squad and I had to establish our own camp in the forest, in fact, it was a true school of life.

One day, we had to return to the base, but on foot. The truck that was driving us had left the day before, it was snowing a lot, and without delay, we had packed our bags and taken the road, missing 15 km, some would say it's a joke, in summer, we could consider this as a healthy walk , but just try to do it on snow that slows down the steps considerably. The rangers were soaked and seemed to weigh several kilos, about 30 cm of snow, the further we went, the more we got stuck.

The instructors had asked us to stay in a T-shirt, equipped with all the equipment we used to set up the camp, our backpacks with all our sleeping and changing equipment, the helmet covering the upper part like a cherry on a cake, and the rifle strap covering our shoulder.

Little by little we were advancing on this snow-covered ground, with sore feet and all the equipment that weighed on our backs. Our T-shirts were wet, and the strap of our gun rubbed them, causing irritation. During the night, we had slept very little, each had to do his turn. We were in bad shape to entangle this march, which seemed interminable, physically and mentally, I was trying. What has allowed us to maintain ourselves is this inner strength, which manifests itself more frequently in extreme cases, leaving us no other option but to move on.

When you look inside yourself for all the necessary resources, everything is still possible. Take one step and then the next, thinking that we are almost there.

In this little anecdote, I'm going to ask you this simple question. "*Why the hell do you give up so close to the goal?*".

I will not repeat my whole book "*Guaranteed Success*", but I can provide you with information that will serve you all your life: "*Never be overwhelmed by external events!*".

Whatever the situation, you should not allow yourself to sink. Of course your situation is too difficult to solve, of course it seems insurmountable, but if you change your thinking, you will prevent your boat from taking water before the boat reaches its destination in the promised land.

If I have some very good advice for you, never speak in terms of "*Problems*"! Delete this from your psychological list and replace it with the term "*Solutions*"!

At work, do not be impressed by the mass of documents on your desk, be methodical and say to yourself: "*Where do I start?*" The great leaders of this world never find a problem, and if they ever want to get there to be, do what they do! act accordingly without worrying about the difficulty, if you see the wall, find a way to get over it or overcome it.

It's difficult, I understand, but it's mostly because you listen too much to your little inner voice, too used to your old beliefs, you know that despite all the difficulties of life, there is always a solution, and conversely, every advantage hides a part of the drawbacks.

The law of balance

This is the main law that is directly related to the phenomenon of attractiveness, and it is the important phase of the reprogramming of the subconscious mind.

We attract to ourselves what we think and feel. But your mind, too used to seeing only the bad side of things, does not believe it too much. In addition, some will not dare to try the experience of change, because they are too dominated by fear, immersed in a comfort zone, that is, the correct sufficiency of our existence, metro, work, dream, in other words, routine. There is this dominant fear of reaching others, and through your eyes, you have a negative perception of yourself, and it will be read on your face.

Have you ever wondered if it was they who lacked confidence? What if they are jealous? It is difficult for you to perceive it, because you are focused on yourself and the fear of being judged.

While if you imagine others as your equals, you will attract them to you trying to understand what is happening in their heads, there will be a phenomenon of psychic conciliation.

Why am I telling you all this? Because in the world in which we live, we all have an ego (huge or not), and we all need to be loved and considered.

Take the situation the other way around, if you have a person in front of you who is interested in who you are, who understands your problems, it will seem empathic, the perception you will have is sympathy. Would not you like to be that guy appreciated for who he is?

When you ignore everyone, bring everything back to be noticed and spend your time criticizing others, do not be surprised to be ignored in turn, criticized and seen as selfish. In the opposite direction, how would you see this person if he or she came to you?

The interior must "*sweat*" outward, both outwards and inwards, everything that is contemplated, the people that meet, the events that occur, all of which come from the real world (the exterior) have a direct impact on the subconscious.

What some will perceive as good, will not be perceived by everyone. We ourselves, in relation to our resentment towards the outside world, and "sweat" towards others.

The same is true for events, your environment and the things you have, you make an incorrect estimate of them. Love what you have, feel the richness of this world, there is a lot of treasure to discover, consider that every event in your life can have a positive impact. Become rich internally in culture, in knowledge of the world, you still have so many beautiful years to live, so many to discover, when you see what I would call "*profit*" or "*benefit*", your natural magnetism will attract to you everything you desire , the good people, the good events, and the long-awaited objects.

There is balance from the moment your thoughts of the subconscious mind align with the outside world, for better or for worse. To put it simply, for those who know the expressions "*see the glass half empty*" or "*see the glass half full*", you have to see the symbolism in it. When you think it is empty, you think negatively, because your subconscious mind is oriented toward deprivation. Whereas if you see it half full, it will be oriented towards wealth, profit.

The world around us is the same for everyone, what is changing is the perception we have of it for good or for bad. Some time ago you have become used to being in a pattern of negativity and lack that everything you are currently reading seems absurd, is the truth that gives you your subconscious, what happens when you think you have no luck, that everything you try It will never work, because your life has accustomed you to this inner conviction.

To prove it, for example, when you work and they inform you of the salary you will receive, you have the security of having this amount at the end of the month, this expectation is a certainty, your mind is right and happy with this salary, it is true and clear that this will happen, it is a true future event, but when you are supposed to win a million euros, it is a fictional future, it is the imagination that works, even if you imagine it hard, it will not happen, because inside you There is an intimate conviction.

As in games of chance, the odds of winning sums ranging from € 1 to € 30 are more frequent than winning € 5,000. Why? Because there is a difference between what you can earn and what you want to get more, one is oriented towards the habitual sufficiency of your mind, is familiar with this truth, does a job, or even asks for social assistance, is in action. When leaving your comfort zone to get more is also in action, and especially in interaction.

It is easier for you to access what is true, it is your subconscious mind that affirms it, not only that you will only have those quantities, but that you have never had luck, in your interior, it is an affirmation.

It is very important to remember what I am saying to you on these lines, you will understand why some people are lucky, while others are still working hard to obtain a scarce income and feel unfortunate.

Is that these people that you see in your life have oriented their minds towards sufficiency and abundance, are happy with what they have, happy in life, while others are unhappy because they are not satisfied with what they have and always want more, they are always in need, a new television, a house, a sports car, there is nothing wrong with having dreams come true, but when you are unhappy in your life, it is first because you have become accustomed to jealousy and envy, there is a way to jealousy, often to criticize those who manage alone, but I do not say this for everyone. Certainly it will tell me, there are rich families and children can enjoy their wealth, I would answer that precisely, they have been immersed for a long time in this sociocultural scheme, wealth has always been present in their lives, they are satisfied with what they have.

Others fought and firmly believed in what they were doing, Soprano, Charles Aznavour, Line Renaud, Florent Pagny, they had the intimate conviction that they achieved it by believing in themselves, nothing was easy for them, but they clung with a mood oriented to abundance, they had something to contribute, a voice, a message to send. If they had stayed at home and complained, saying to themselves, "*It's too hard, I can not do it*", do you think they would have left a mark on the earth? And you, what do you have to bring to this world? They knew their situation and were happy despite what they had, their joy, their enthusiasm sweated outside. They have embarked on careers that we know with the intimate and profound conviction that they will succeed.

As a writer, my desire is to take a message to as many people as possible, I put myself in the place of the reader who wants to discover answers, I am not oriented to the need to sell my book for money but to share what I already have inside, I have knowledge and experiences that I would like to share, that is my goal as an author.

Enjoy what you have and the world around you, stop complaining and do not do not limit your mind to a comfort zone that you do not like! Have a goal in mind with the firm belief that it will work, eliminate the barriers of doubt and fear.

This sums up the law of balance, changing the perception of the outside world within you. You are rich and everyone has something to contribute to the greatest number of people.

Do not behave like a poor person, always in need, with your hand extended upwards, asking for help or complaining about your condition, and acting like a rich man who does not need anything and who benefits from the riches of this world, be happy with what You have, although it is not ideal for you, reconsider the events, the things that surround you, and you will have a new look on everything that surrounds you, both in human relationships and in energy, give it to those who are under you , needy, and the world will look at you in another way, your aura will shine, what you will release from yourself will only be positive. If you are rich inside, you will be rich on the outside cultivating a new state of mind.

The law of knowledge

The television is on BFMTV, a continuous news channel, in the news there is a demonstration in the Greater Lille about the plans of restructuring of a tire factory, the staff is very worried about their future. The Prime Minister is on course to negotiate with the unions, arrives by car under the booing of the employees, as soon as he has arrived, is glorified with all the names of the birds, having to make his way, is immediately interrogated by the journalists on the terrain:

- Minister, what is the purpose of your visit?
- We have taken the full scope of the issue, and I have come personally on behalf of the government to negotiate with the parties involved

(unions and construction managers).
- What answers would you like to give to all employees of the plant?
- They will be discussed in the interview that I will have in a few minutes about the reclassification of some workers.

In this brief response, the Prime Minister moves to the place of negotiations with the unions and those responsible for the works, and the entire interview will be communicated to the employees.

A reduction of 20% in the personnel was considered, but this figure was reported by 10%. This part of the staff will have a reclassification plan, while others will only have to register as unemployed.

Only then, those who remain will be the main actors of the factory, a handful of workers, and the rest will represent the managers, executives and the leader.

These same workers who were unemployed no longer had any vision of the future, most of whom only knew this company since adolescence, and did not even see themselves in another place, because they expected to stay until retirement.

Their only point of reference was this factory, or they no longer wanted to go to work elsewhere, or they lacked the necessary knowledge. Most of them have stopped studying very early and have never had the opportunity to write a cover letter or a curriculum vitae. They had very little knowledge in other trades, no experience in other places. Very few have continued reading books to enrich their knowledge, the latter have been saved thanks to it, have regained the advantage over the situation.

When we fail to learn, apart from reading VSD or Paris Match (I do not see how Prince William's marriage would help in any way in a great majority of situations), we feel ignorant, we tend to stop thinking "*why bother?*"

But on the other hand, when we enrich our knowledge, our inner strength grows. We feel that we can overcome events, so that the impossible becomes possible. Read books to learn economics, science, French or mathematics is always important in this world, gives the feeling of being less void.

This thing that many people say is "it's boring!" Others say to themselves, fortunately, that I've recovered, and it's never too late to control things, nothing is lost, unless our sub-conscious mind takes us to believe it

Also, I'll tell you something, talking about programs, for those who watch TV shows like "Les douze coups de midi" by Jean Luc Reichmann, there was a player named Christian Quesada who won almost € 800,000 before being dethroned by a candidate, 193 performances in the program, he was nicknamed "the teacher", but where did all this knowledge come from? Christian Quesada had many problems, he was unemployed at the time of his first presentation, but he was a very educated person, which allowed him to be selected for the show.

For those who have never paid attention to this detail, how many people of the working class have participated in this program? Very few, compared to teachers, directors or senior managers.

This is not because the chain denigrates the world of the working class, and much less, it is mainly because, before appearing in this type of program, there are always screening tests before obtaining what could be called the famous " *sesame audiovisual* ", do you think this example speaks?

Now you know what you have to do, do not be afraid to open books, even if you do not share all the opinions of the authors (because each one thinks differently), varying your readings, you will have a solid base of knowledge, and you will be able to take advantage again in all situations.

Another situation that I learned from the lucky winners of the game, those who became millionaires because of them, did not stay that way for a long time, why? most of them did not have the notion of money, it was a new situation and they lost control, they made risky investments without any knowledge, they tried hard to share family and friends (it is legitimate), but not only brought happiness, among the wars of clans in the bosom of the family and the friends who cheated them under the pretext that they had become selfish because they did not give enough according to them, and not all, there are also people of bad intentions promising quite expensive investments in real estate whose color they did not even see, nor money, nor the good in question, the thieves took advantage of their knowledge to exploit the mentally weak, with little information read on the internet, they found themselves after a while with a residue that no longer allowed them bring a great lifestyle, also burned the candle at both ends, is like giving a box of matches to a child, ends up burning his fingers.

If I had to give you some advice, if by the most curious coincidence (you never know), you earn a lot of money, you keep discreet and informed! Avoid telling your friends or relatives, or not revealing all the content of your small fortune. This is information that should only be personal.

And also, if you want to keep your place at work, be able to retrain, find one for those who do not have it, try to participate in games shows or even make good placements with the right people, educate yourself! There is no age to start, there is no age to finish (except in a fir box, but that's another story).

The law of continuity

For the youngest, who entered the professional life a few years ago, they can always return to school, the benefits do not disappear as well, but the knowledge runs out over time, because several years pass and the older ones add new information, dominating everything what you have learned

Let me explain to you that you have a very important document on your desk that you have taken care to memorize, on top of it, another document completely different from the first, which you must also read, these are achievements.

Next, a large file is placed in the first two documents, files, internal notes, you should know everything about these latest arrivals.

One day, during a meeting, a client asks you to talk to him about the first case. You look in your file in vain, but you can not find it, you have pieces and pieces, but you are afraid to give information, because in the meantime, you had to read other files.

This is what happened, the achievements you had, you did not see them again and you went on to something else, never felt that you were coming out of it, until the fateful day when they asked you to talk about a subject as old as Erod.

Why? Because there was no continuity with the first document that you memorized.

Another example: You have a black wall with drawn drawings in front of you, you look at it for years until the day you decide to paint it white with a poor quality paint, the first layer will be dark gray, the second will be medium gray, the third will be light gray, and the fourth, even clearer to finish with a broken white, you will need a lot of paint to cover everything. Now you are getting used to the white wall, and you would like to remember the patterns that were there to play on this wall. However, it is impossible to remember exactly where these patterns were, you should have drawn the contours of them in each layer to keep a visible trace.

Your memory is the same, you remember everything from the moment you keep a certain continuity. When your attention is relaxed on something else (a white wall), and you've been looking at it for years, it's impossible to remember the patterns. For this reason, nothing should be taken for granted and memory can only be worked on.

The law of repetition

We all have in mind a song that comes to mind, some easier than others given its text length, the shorter it is, the more we remember it.

For this passage, and in accordance with the

current events, which I am trying to do, let us take the example of the singer *Jaïn*. Write lyrics with melodies that remain recorded in consciousness for a long time, the last one is called "*Alright*", whose words and regular rhythm is easily impregnated in the memory, becomes a loop "*Things gonna be alright, things gonna be just fine*" . Listening to it only two or three times, it is recorded, and we also hum at times. The subconscious easily accepted this non-aggressive music from the awareness that it returns at any time of the day.

This was the case of *Patrick Hernández* with the famous "*Born to be alive*" or the title of *Village People* "*YMCA*" whose titles are still being broadcast, and for more than forty years as I write this line.

Just to show you that very short and repeated information reaches us more easily than the longer information, because it does not require a great effort of memory, when we compare songs with text, we also remember it, by the force of conscious repetition. It is precisely this repetition that makes these music acquired.

To this, we add knowledge and continuity, and you have the first ingredients to maintain knowledge, but also to feel that something seems easy, because you always know.

Our brain is a fabulous tool when we know how to use it, it can contain billions of information per second, I do not mean that its resources are unlimited, but they are very vast.

Do not be afraid to learn and increase your knowledge, keep and practice everything you have learned, do not skimp on knowledge, although at first sight it seems complicated, your subconscious mind will better accept the entry of new information if you maintain a certain continuity.

Knowledge opens the doors of an infinite world, you can be everything you've always dreamed of. Now I go to the fifth law, the law of perseverance.

The law of perseverance

I will illustrate with this little story:

A long time ago, in a distant land, was "the mountain of difficulties". Next to her was a village where the inhabitants lived in his shadow.

Nobody knew what was hidden behind this

huge mountain, the villagers were as lifeless, they did not know the enthusiasm, the place where they lived was synonymous with sadness.

One day, one of them had a vision, imagined vast green plains, bathed by the rays of a luminous star, and was right behind this mountain. He was a fragile young man, but sure of himself.

Then, without the right equipment, he decided to attack the immensity of this rocky dome, began with what fell, and hit constantly, night and day, with stones in the facade. 5000 times, 10000 times, continued again and again......

The inhabitants of the city took him for a fool and took pity on him. However, looking at him helplessly, they brought sustenance. Some prayed for him to stop, so that it would not do any good to disturb, so that the rock would not move a millimeter, and yet the young man continued to hit with stones on the mountain.

The months passed and he was still trying to break the rock, he became strong and his blows became stronger. If he had to count all the blows he gave, he would count himself millions and millions of times, but he still conti-

nued, as if that were his only goal in life. Again and again, it hit, and suddenly, there was a shock, the ground began to tremble, it came from the mountain of difficulties. The inhabitants were afraid and took refuge in their homes, but what they did not see is this mountain that showed the first signs of fragility, the man constantly beat. One last before leaving, thinking it was time to leave. The mountain began to collapse under a cloud of dust. Once the danger was eliminated, the inhabitants abandoned their homes and discovered for the first time a luminous star that they called the sun.

When you are involved in your project, nothing should stop you, not even moments of discouragement. As the young man in the short story, never give up! Even if the first signs are not visible, each small gesture brings you closer to your goal. Even a mountain of difficulties can not withstand repeated blows, in the first place, it becomes brittle, the cracks are not visible yet, but they are there.

In moments of doubt, keep the course, that's the most important thing. No matter what they say, the inhabitants of the brave villages will always dissuade you from stopping, just listen to your heart, if I have to remind you, it is your life, not the lives of others.

Remember all that I just mentioned and all the ingredients that can lead you to success, that is, balance, knowledge, continuity, repetition and perseverance.

Your subconscious is like a mountain to be knocked down, I have never hidden it would be difficult, those who say otherwise will sell you dreams, but you have to stay on land.

Whatever happens, and depending on your level of difficulty, never give up! It is the heavy burden, the price to pay for success.

All those who started from nothing, and who have done very well in life, have not done so simply by snapping their fingers.

You must be able to convince your subconscious to accept the new information provided, read a lot, philosophy, history, geography .... There is no small or big knowledge, there is simply knowledge.

CHAPTER 3: YOUR SUBCONSCIOUS MIND AGAINST THE OUTER WORLD

«I returned to my memory to childhood, to re-discover the feeling of sovereign protection. There is no protection for men. Once you are a man, we will let you go. »
(Antoine de Saint-Exupéry)

Its environment

Your environment is part of you, because it evolves with the *"metro, work, sleep"*, when you go to the Internet, go to work, do your shopping, in fact, it is so modeled in this environment that you do things unconsciously.

It is your daily life and it will be difficult to adapt to another environment, if you were on a desert island (we do not know how), or in nature, you would be lost, far from your modern comfort, your TV or your Smartphone.

Far from buying at the supermarket, you'll have to find out what you need to survive, and in addition to watching documentaries or reading books on the subject, putting it into practice is another story, you'll have to improvise.

If we take the problem in the opposite direction, the case of individuals living in a wild environment, there will be no reference in their subconscious to our own technology, they will resemble Christmas children discovering their gifts, awakening their curiosity, but also his ignorance. How is it possible for men and women to communicate with what looks like a black rectangle on the ear or with their eyes fixed on it?

The words "*text message*", "*email*", "*iPhone*" are totally strange to them, because they do not appear in their references from their subconscious.

But over time, they will learn about these words and their uses, since they will have entered into an unconscious learning process. They will register this new information in their minds and, once they have tested our technology, it will be difficult for them to return to their original environment, intoxicated by our social environment.

On the other hand, they will always be able to survive in a hostile environment, which is an achievement of their lives.

The contrasts

While walking the streets of Cannes, I was able to make a surprising observation.

On television, we only see strasses and glitter, there are some, but not only that. The world of Cannes seemed very contrasted, apart from La croisette with its beautiful hotels and luxury boutiques, there is also poverty. If you ever have the opportunity to go there, unless you have already done so, walking by, you will notice an evident social gap.

Well-dressed couples, the woman in a Chanel suit and the husband in an Armani suit wandering the streets among the poor who beg. My perception was surprising, what placed me between these two situations, between rich and poor, the middle class citizen. He gets to wonder how we would perceive these individuals if we were from one side or another of these social environments.

Of course, wealth or poverty would not be seen in my face, frequenting large hotels, but if I had their eyes, my vision would probably be different.

Our environment changes over time

Our vision of the world changes over time, it is

like looking at an adult as a child, we see him as an adult, and older people appear to be younger as they grow up, without paying more attention.

We realize the physical changes of someone when we stop seeing him for a while, a trip that lasts a year, for example, and then on the way back, you see that same person, it seems it has taken ten years. Our subconscious mind was used to seeing this person, listening to his voice, seeing the features of his face, we did not underestimate him, because over time, our vision gets used to these changes, we have had, without realizing it, aged with he, and that causes a shock by saying "*he's gotten old!* »

Sociocultural codes

Now, suppose you want to be rich (few would not be, unless I'm wrong), how would you re-act in this new situation?

That is to say, and it is not a mystery, that any social group has what are called "*codes*" (of dress, cultural or others). We all have a cultural pattern, when we get up, when we go to work, the company we have, our way of being and the places we frequent, etc ... All this forms our own "*codes*".

It would be difficult to adapt to a comfortable environment without knowing the bases, beginning by frequenting it and learning from its "*codes*".

Now imagine what you would do if you had 1 million euros in your power. Coming from a poor and rich environment where poverty and problems are around you, your reaction would be to make donations to charities or invest that money to make it grow, but specifically, what would you do if this really happened?

A beautiful morning, you discover in your mailbox a letter, error or not on the part of the notary, you do not even ask yourself the question, your name appears on the letter after all, you rush to open it and there is the cold shower.

In the last line, you see a note that says "*due sum: 1 million euros*", but instead of suffering a heart attack in the center of the hall of your building, your eyes are placed on the body of the mail and you read that your distant uncle died left you the sum of 1 000 000 euros. At the same time, you learn that you also have a distant uncle, the surprise is double.

Then comes a very strong enthusiasm, you even want to kiss the janitor Mrs. Gossip, whose desire I doubt she is in the same mood, unless I make a mistake here too.

What to do with this million euros? Before that, your generous soul had resorted to the "*Restos du Coeur*", becoming *Mother Teresa* or *Abbé Pierre*, had even planned a peaceful retreat in the monastery of Luberon (when you would have discovered if it existed and where it was), to begin to raise goats and prepare processed cheeses *"it's so cute!"* or to have planned to invest their money in the bank *Radin* at an interest rate that could deceive even a Parisian tourist on holiday in Haute-Savoie who wanted to eat a steak with Provencal sauce in a traditional restaurant

In fact, if you get a check like that, I'd be in shock, why?

What do you think should be the first thing you should do? Keep it? Not without taking some precautions, leaving a trace ... a photocopy and the email that accompanies it? Buy insurance and install a safe in the center of your 20 m² studio? This amount would attract attention. In fact, it would surprise you so much that you did not know where to start, you would lose the information, you would see a lot in your life, a situation that had never happened before. In your head, is the crisis of 1929 or the year 2000's bug, with the question "*WHAT TO DO?*".

Since the connection between your point of origin and this new information is not created, it is lost.

Their references can be summarized in eating pasta Bolognese four times a week, which is nothing compared to the menu offered at the Hilton, of course.

The only thing that is certain is that in your current environment, you have control, all the elements you need are in your subconscious, with references to your experience, we add an element, you would be like this individual discovering mobile phones and emails, it is new information that will be processed, over time, this novelty will be part of you if your mind is ready to accept it. If this is the case, these new technologies will be part of your subconscious mind.

Shyness and stuttering

Now that you have assimilated the "*master*"

principle of the flow of information in our sub-conscious, I was not going to finish this book without mentioning the causes of communication disorders related to social and emotional conditioning.

The shyness, therefore, is a lack of self-confidence, in relation to the events experienced with a group of individuals, comes from childhood, but this can end in adulthood due to an emotional shock. The subject of this discomfort has been in the past victim of intimidation, threats that have attacked his psyche, so he does not communicate or communicate little fear of the reactions, regardless of the person in front of him. He has assimilated a pattern of behavior in a generalized way and freezes fear inside him.

We have all had in our lives our "*great Lulu*", who was making us have a hard time with his gang, this character, you recorded it in your subconscious, and in your life, it seems that you meet the "*great Lulu*" everywhere, or at least with individuals who remind you of it.

You want to appear in the open, but a star obscures your thoughts, an emotional memory that makes you doubt it, because you are afraid of mockery, of being laughed at, so your creative power and your opinions remain silent, wandering to always in the unconscious (your inner world). Why? Because you have simply assimilated as true, everything you have been told, that you are null, unreflective, good for nothing, but believing in it, you are only living the lives of others, or at least the life they have decided for you , But at what moment do you do it for yourself? It's your life, and it's up to you to build it.

I assure you, if you wish, that this situation is not permanent, only if you decide to "let go" of the disturbing events of your youth, and create a new perception of the human race.

This is also found in stuttering, which is a disorder of expression.

You want to transmit a message, exchange opinions on any topic, but when it comes to expressing it, the shadow of the great Lulu appears. Stuttering is a psychological disorder that occurs in two phases. In the first place, the subject wants to give his opinion, when he expresses it, there is a psychological block, that of the cause and the effect. Your strong inner anticipates the mockery. On the one hand, you want to say things and, on the other, your subconscious mind stops this impulse by whispering: "*Beware! Remember the fat Lulu!* »

There is a crossing of two information elements that come out of the subconscious, one expressive and the other restrictive, as if we were simultaneously pressing the accelerator and the brake and asking "*Is this good or bad?*" Then your inner strength says "*Ok, I'll do it!*", A mental confusion between Doubt and courage provoke leaps of elocution.

Information, ego and perception

While you walk in an art gallery, you find yourself facing Victor Lotin, one of your old acquaintances, who you have not seen since high school.

He comes to you, very happy to see you again, but this joy is not shared, to know the odious character, unprecedented heaviness, is always the first to expose his science, praises an artist in front of a canvas listeners, your steps turn outward, desperately seeking a way to escape to escape the individual. The impression has remained as it is in your memories.

People can change as much as they want, but not the image given at the time they met, this, in their mind, remains the same. You have to adapt to this new behavior. It is not impossible, but sometimes it takes time, just as your environment has to adapt to you, it is called the "*mirror effect*".

The inculcated beliefs

They are like serpents that bite you and whose poison invades your whole body. Determine who you are internally, a person unmotivated, discouraged, insubstantial, because your subconscious has accepted as true everything that has been said since your early childhood, the starting point of your entire existence. In another context, if your life has been supported, animated and maximized, your mind will be oriented towards success, in this case, if nobody has done it for you, then do it for yourself, you know what you are worth inside, Depending on what you create, the subconscious mind will give you a direction to follow by the force of the conviction that will be anchored in you.

If, for example, you are going to see a clairvoyant and she tells you that you will become rich, famous and that you will know your soul mate, it is very unlikely that this will happen, because your subconscious mind is conditioned differently, it will have an effect negative, because in your interior it is very contradictory with what you have assimilated in your inner being.

On the other hand, if you go back to her and tell her that everything she predicted did not work out making a scandal in the middle of her consultation, she will threaten you with the bad luck that your life will be nothing but misery and loneliness. You will have this idea of a hex in mind.

You will be tempted to believe in it in the depths of yourself, because for the subconscious mind, everything will seem coherent, in other words, you will create your own misfortune, and it is all that you have assimilated and believed that will give strength to this curse. Even more so if, for example, it slips on the damp ground, receives a pot on the head or meets a black cat, which are in fact only events that can occur in everyday life, but that will reinforce the belief of a curse .

Everything that happens inside your being, materializes outside, you are one with the universe around you, what gives strength to the curse are your beliefs, the fruit of your subconscious. You attract to yourself all the misfortunes that you think according to the law of balance.

To get out of this spiral, you will have to redirect your thoughts to healthier beliefs, to the wealth and prosperity of the world.

Your life changes when your beliefs change, you are not a victim of any destiny, except the fruit of your subconscious mind.

When a tile, a flat tire, a blocking machine and other similar events push you to say "I'm not lucky", this statement is bad luck. Do not make your mind more unhappy and redirect it to happiness, it will only be better. The problems happen, but they only last a moment if you do not mind.

When you think positively, good things happen in your life, you attract to yourself what you think.

You are not yet aware of the potential within you, in fact, the brain is a huge generator that gives shape to our whole life, it has immense powers, including that of creativity. It works with everything that can be provided, its reserves are endless.

If you fall, you stand up and keep going, take small "*huge*" steps to do it, because whatever you do towards the final goal (your success), whether through small or larger things, your goal is already less far than the day before.

CHAPTER 4: AWAKENING OF THE UNCONSCIOUS MIND

"We always want the imagination to be the capacity to form images. However, it is rather the ability to distort the images provided by perception, it is above all the ability to free ourselves from raw images, to change images. »
(Gaston Bachelard)

The imagination

Our brain is a wonderful tool, it allows us to feel emotions related to our five senses, record information, synthesize with them, but beyond that, it gives us a fabulous power, that of the imagination that allows us to reinvent ourselves or feel good when events external causes make us suffer.

Use existing elements in our subconscious to build new situations in an unreal world, images that shape our dreams, because the desired feeling is pleasure.

The unconscious is our world, a protective bubble surrounds it so as not to reveal the least of our thoughts, and the subconscious serves as a valve since, of course, it contains information that allows us to reveal them or not, it is the judge of our thoughts.

For example, at this moment I am writing a book, and my imagination is built in my unconscious, the conscious gives the external information and the subconscious treats it making a transcription in the real world (writing).

The subconscious provides ideas to the unconscious, derived from ancient information, gives matter to my imagination. It is like a construction game, the more elements you des, the more accurate the object or thought you want to externalize.

Do you remember when you played in the Lego? You take a square (new information) and try to combine it with a rectangle already in your possession (old information), which gives it a new shape that will be evocative. We can imagine a bus, a train or a car, depending on what the subconscious mind provides the unconscious.

It is through the unconscious that lies are built or a life is invented that we do not have, but if we can convince our subconscious that this false existence is ours, it will eventually accept it.

The unconscious, if it has the power to build, can be destructive, because when a department manager bothers you, in your imagination, you want to hit it (honestly, who would have ever thought it?), But this fictional universe can become the own reality is what happens with psychopaths, character traits begin to reappear as soon as the subconscious accepts data and value judgments that drown in them. At first, this is characterized by a sense of confusion.

The morality that you were taught in your childhood prevents you from acting, and on the other hand, new information created in the form of neuroassociated stimuli, creating an alternative reality in the unconscious. It seems so real and detailed that mental confusion is created.

Mnemonic referencing

The mnemonic is called a point of reference that helps to establish the connection between the presented object and our subconscious.

This can be by size, shape, color or function, for example, we associate the fire extinguisher with its utility to extinguish a fire, red and of a certain size, it can be water or powder, in the second smaller case.

The mnemonic also helps us find our way in space, that is, a place. We go to a city thanks to signs, panels, buildings, trees ... Their shapes and colors are immediately evocative, when you ask someone for your route, the town hall, the post office, the church, etc. tell you.

These are data that we all know and all you have to do is find the evocative forms of these buildings.

Mnemonics also work when you have to remember a word, if you remember when you were a child, you still use it to learn foreign languages, looking for a close term, for example, in french, to say red, you use "rouge", you think of it color of the bottle of wine.

Our creative power is unlimited and comes from the right hemisphere of our brain, it is our inner world where the imagination resides. This is where dreams and ideas are made with the information gathered by the conscience, and the information retained by our subconscious mind.

In the phase of deep sleep

The subconscious remains very active, but no longer communicates directly with the conscious path, closing the eyes, closing the doors that lead to the outside world, and the subconscious takes over. The neural connections with their external environment are interrupted.

From that moment, you are in your bubble, the memories that are in your subconscious communicate with your creative mind and take us to an ideal world, based on the information collected during your workday, for example.

When I was younger, the teachers recommended that we learn the lessons at night. Several years ago it was discovered that students who reviewed the previous day were more likely to pass their exams than most students who preferred to play video games, watch movies on television at night or play outdoor soccer, and These same students had the bad habit of studying in the morning.

As a result, the lesson was certainly learned, but temporarily inscribed in the subconscious mind, because it had not adapted to a significant change in the memory bank, the effects were felt during the test exams, plagued by memory gaps, even if the clues to the answers were in the question of the subject.

In effect, the assimilation of new information can only be done under two conditions, the level of involvement in the subject, that is, whether the student is interested or not in what is presented, whether or not only a text or a mathematical formula that you know by heart, your mind must be constantly curious about everything, why use such a formula, how to apply it. But also, learning is governed by the law of repetition, if neural connections are like electric lines, a single pulse does not light a lamp, the mind will not be "illuminated".

You can imagine, memory can hold no more than 10% of what happens in a day, difficult to remember every spoken word, places visited or the face of someone you see for the first time, consciousness needs to provide details to your subconscious that you need to satisfy yourself, if you do not, it will happen the same as when you do not feed your body, lose weight and weaken, unable to *"lift books"*, the data will become increasingly technical, especially in today's progressive society in day.

The most dangerous thing is also to leave your mind without training, for example, if some time ago you had studied mathematics, then it seemed easier than now, do you remember how to apply a rule of three? The square of the hypotenuse? The first and second degree equations? Looking at a math book, you would be surprised at what you have lost in knowledge.

Some will say that mathematics is useless in today's world, I will answer the same thing that many teachers will probably tell you, that it is used to train your brain and maintain a logical mind.

In my previous professions as a storekeeper, it was useful for me to apply addition, subtraction, multiplication, in particular, I remember having used table 9 several times when I had to put the products on palettes.

Education and training will make you a better person, because what happens inside is perceived outside, and it is normal that some individuals seem stupid, because they believe they have acquired enough knowledge, but these are fears applied, neither through training, nor in everyday life where situations lead us to use them.

The conscious plays an important role, allows to provide new information by making neuro-associated combinations, it falls asleep when the information is already known. The point of union is therefore between the unconscious mind and the subconscious mind, which is a bit treacherous, because by advancing in life, having only this point of reference, it can be diluted, transformed by our unconscious mind, which It also shows that the subconscious mind can be reprogrammed by the situations of everyday life, you have stayed the same as several years ago, but with new thoughts, imagine that 20 years ago, do you still see yourself studying? In a classroom? Can you still feel the emotions you felt when you entered the classroom? Difficult, because you live in your current environment, not in the past. Your subconscious has received new instructions.

If I take the example of the lesson to be learned again, if it is done in a robotic way, we give matter to our subconscious mind without the information being processed either by neuroassociated stimuli or by our emotions.

When you learn a text in french, you do it by association with a english equivalent of each word.

For example, if you have to translate "*The cat eat the mouse*" from English to French, you do it like this:

THE | CAT | EAT | THE | MOUSE
Neuroassociation
LE | CHAT | MANGE | LA | SOURIS

The information processed in the subconscious will be recorded in your memories, shortly after this information processing, everything will seem natural, only collecting the data already collected.

Therefore, and to return to the phase of deep sleep, it is better to learn a lesson the day before, because it is during the resting phase (interruption with the outside world), when the unconscious makes its small sauce from the ingredients of the subconscious, that can combine with each other without a coherent order, creating fantastic worlds.

The brain is a wonderful tool, as I said before, because it has the ability to take information, validate it, then transcribe it to the unconscious, and make it validate by the subconscious, the valve of our thoughts. It is the collective unconscious that has made it possible to know the world in which we live, the great inventions of historical figures that have allowed us to evolve and that have opened the doors of the objects that we use in our daily life, without the invention of the printing press , we would continue dealing with manuscripts.

Archimedes, Galileo, Leonardo da Vinci, Newton, Thomas Edison, all have made a contribution to the world through their creative spirit, having learned never to surrender in the collective interest.

Not all the great inventions have appeared by themselves, and come from the same place common to all, our brains.

 What would have happened if the great creators of this world had not received any instruction? You probably would not read this book, the Internet would not exist, because I use it to make myself known on social networks. Understand this, your greatest wealth is in you, what you will do with it depends only on you, feed your subconscious, maintain it, give it the material on which you can work with your unconscious, you are your own creator, that of your destiny.

This truth is universal, remember it well! *YOU BECOME WHAT YOU THINK!* to quote Descarte's words "I think, so I am!"

Not only in the way he thinks, but also in what

you want, how others think of you! How you want to be perceived and how you perceive yourself!

The excesses of the unconscious

If the unconscious can build, it can also destroy, the perception of the world is altered, the interactions with the outside world are negative, as I explained, what comes from within "*sweats*" out, by gestures, facial expressions, and by the inconsistent words that are pronounced, the individuals that suffer from psychological pathologies or a misinterpretation of the external world, perceive all as enemies, to want to control them.

Here is a story that I have been told recently. This happened a few years ago during the Christmas season in New York City, a large shopping mall had opened for the holidays, and families were plentiful in the aisles, going from stores to stores. Suddenly, they heard like thunder, most of the customers jumped because they did not expect such noise. Then a second detonation. Fear won in the gallery, cries of terror were heard, people in the building were paralyzed by fear, others fled and sought a hiding place.

A policeman was present, the only one in this terrified crowd, was not on duty, but with his wife to go shopping. Fortunately for him and for the terrified clients, he kept his service weapon and his badge.

It was located on the top floor of the gallery, hidden behind a pole, near the railing and looked right under it. He saw a man armed with a shotgun shooting at everything that moved, both people running and the curtains fluttering.

The vigils were on the ground, alive or dead, no one dared to go check it, because the crazy shooter was nearby.

Suddenly, the man saw the policeman and shot him, who arrived at the station where he was hiding. The policeman asked for slow reinforcements, followed by shots in the gallery until the arrival of the police, who found a butcher shop under his feet.

Eventually they found and shot the mad shooter, the ambulances were in place and the wounded were taken care of. Many people who have suffered a psychological shock have had difficulty recovering from this ordeal, and are still victims of this mad shooter. They are currently in therapy to forget this painful passage.

What happened in the mind of that crazy shooter and who was he?

I will not praise him, given the human drama he has caused, his mind was disconnected from reality, his consciousness altered and his imagination (the unconscious) completely abandoned his internal environment. What he saw came from his imagination, validated by the subconscious mind.

This guy played a lot of videogames, and this virtual world had become his reality, he was immersed in another universe. His unconscious controlled his actions.

Another example, always in difficult circumstances. In California, a couple had been living in harmony for more than ten years.

Overnight, the husband showed signs of psychological distress, made incoherent comments, supposedly because his father-in-law wanted to kill him and because he had raped his children. His wife was beginning to be afraid that his partner would threaten her with screaming at first, insisting that everything he said was true until he succeeded in causing trouble in his wife's mind.

Both filed complaints against the wife's father for threats of death and contact with minors, which led to the conviction of the latter, who was surprised by these accusations, denying that he was innocent.

Soon after, the husband, wanting to add something else to his madness, tried to convince his wife that she had also been raped by her own father; he insisted and beat her until she finally accepted her incoherent comments for fear of being beaten, but inside she kept all her lucidity, but what to do in front of a husband who had gone completely crazy?

Shortly afterwards, he told them that his father was a former Russian spy and that he had sent men to shoot him, that he had barricaded himself in his house, and he asked his wife to go and pick up the mail for him, for fear that there would be a sniper hidden.

One day, the husband left the conjugal house, took a few steps and shot himself in the leg. His wife ran and brought him home, he wanted to prove that he was right and that a sniper had shot him.

An investigation revealed that the bullet was fired at close range, leaving the investigators confused, one of them took the woman aside for questioning and asked her if things were going well with her husband. He could only answer his question with a lie, afraid of the reactions of the person with whom he shared his roof.

But this situation was reversed one day, when the husband forced the whole family to leave the premises to escape the sniper fire. They all packed their bags and got into the car. The man asked to his wife to take them to the house of one of her friends, but she did not know the address, so they went around the city. The husband lost patience and stopped. He pulled one of the children out and forced him to kneel; He took his gun and pointed to the head of his own son.

The woman in panic tried to convince him to calm down and help him find his friend's address. She invited him to calm down and go home, for that, he played his game saying that armed men were waiting for him at the destination, and that the safest place for now was his house.

They returned and the woman continued to

make her husband believe that she understood him. She told her that she was going to go to the police to report his father for the "so-called" rape that she suffered as a child and for the assassination attempts, but that at the moment he had to remain hidden, since there are still shooters outside.

The plan worked, and the woman went directly to the police station to see one of the investigators who had suspicions about her husband. She told him the facts, the dementia of her husband, the domestic violence, the innocence of her father, the investigator took her statement and tried to find out a little more about her husband.

Shortly after, he was arrested for domestic violence and sentenced to a very severe sentence, the father of the wife was released from any suspicion.

This story left its aftermath, not only in the woman who underwent the therapy shortly after, but also in the children and the people around who had been helpless and present in the hallucinations of the husband.

What happened in this particular case? This story has psychological similarities with the history of the crazy shooter. Both created a universe for themselves, and their inner world had become their outer world, the associative neurological connections were made between the subconscious and the unconscious that made a reinterpretation of the outside world, which was at the origin of their insanity.

A narcissistic perversion

What we call narcissistic perversion can be summed up in a constant need to want. The narcissistic being is generally a weak person internally and seeks an ideal of life that he would like to lead, so he invents a life for themselves. It is separated from the reality that consciousness provides, it does not think, it interprets through the unconscious, creating a deceptive truth.

This individual always wants more, to be better than others, on the cusp of success, and his strength, from which he gets disparaging others, and will never recognize his limitations and ignorance. Reinvent the history of their lives in a slightly more diluted way. All this for people to be interested in their little person, weak inside.

It is a disease that I consider dramatic, the individual ends alone, because everyone tries to escape from him, so there are two possible options, or he commits suicide or is made to understand otherwise by more violent intentions, because he has that irresistible need to be interested in him.

CHAPTER 5: LIVING IN HARMONY WITH YOUR UNIVERSE

"Being good is being in harmony with yourself. Discord is forced to be in harmony with others."
(Oscar Wilde)

The interior "sweats" to the outside

Everything around us is our universe, it is the same for everyone, regardless of its social or cultural origin, the earth will continue to turn, the night following the day, we all breathe the same air, we drink the same water, and most of the The most powerful people in this world have the same blood type as you. It is the environment in which you operate and you are part of it.

In addition, you are composed of the same elements of this universe that is a multitude of electrons, protons and neutrons, from an atomic point of view, you are part of this environment. This will not change over time, the components of this world simply taking another form, whether solid or liquid, or vaporous, that will make up an element will always be made up of atoms, of different structures, but always with electrons, protons and neutrons.

This same universe is composed of two worlds, one is outside, what we see, touch or hear is part of it, it is the "*incoming*" information. Then there is another, located within ourselves, that interprets according to the oldest information, either consciously or from the unconscious, and there is a point of union between the two, a combination like nesting two cubes of Lego between them, and that will form the "*outgoing*" information.

The first is common to all mortals, a rich man will see the same forest as you, admire the stars and breathe the same air. However, you were taught beliefs and notions of values from an early age, you learned what money and abundance were in a certain way, that having millions of euros is synonymous with wealth and that it was impossible for you to achieve this goal because you came from a modest environment. On the other hand, if an individual is immersed in a comfortable environment, they will retain a sense of abundance, they will have everything they want out of life, they will have the privilege of studying for a long time in secondary schools, their perception will be different from theirs, and yet the universe is exactly the same from the atomic point of view.

This resonated in your subconscious mind, giving you the sensation of a distant goal, almost impossible to reach, and during your education, he whispered to you: "*Why bother? You will never succeed*", looking over you, and thinking that we do not have all that the son of a rich person has, your mind will bathe in "*wanting*", doubting your own value.

So I would answer that we all have exactly the same value in the universe, what changes is the interpretation we make of him in relation to our beliefs, from our inner world, in the way we build it in relation to them.

Let's take a glass of water that contains half the liquid, this represents the universe, and is part of it. A person who lives in abundance will always see the glass half full and will be satisfied with what it has, will be directed upwards to see what is happening below, and will see liquid (goal achieved). While the one who bathes in the lack will always see the glass half empty, will be waiting to have a little more, will be placed at the bottom, and his gaze will go upwards, then he will not see the air (goal not reached). One has both elements, and the other only one (water) and wants to obtain the next one (air).

If the outside world is the same for everyone, the interior of each individual is different, each one will have its own perception, creating beliefs, some limitations, others oriented to progress.

You can not be rich, you already are!

When you understand that you are one with the whole universe, you are already very rich, however, you have been taught false notions about values. For some, being rich means having money, for others, it means living on everything the earth provides.

As it is written in the Bible, "*Everything you ask of God, you must know that you have already obtained it*", "*even before calling, God will have already answered you*", in fact, we feel rich when we know how to be happy that we have and we can appreciate everything that the Earth can provide us in abundance. "*God gives and in abundance*", it suffices to know how to look where it is necessary, healthy writings explain it to us very well, I could cite many passages on the subject, but is not it better to read the Bible yourself? "*If your faith is as big as a mustard seed, everything is possible!*" (Gospel according to Matthew).

By taking this fact into account in our lives, then we follow the right direction, the path to abundance and success. Appreciate everything that the universe offers you, as soon as your feeling is oriented towards abundance, then abundance will come to you, otherwise it is impossible to obtain anything else that the world could provide if you no longer appreciate anything of what you possess. So, "*help yourself and heaven will help you!*" You have an immense power within you that only wants to "*sweat*" outward, that of decision.

The secret power in each one of us

If our minds had the power to attract to us everything we want, it would be fabulous, right? Some have already tried, but they said it did not work, because they misused the law of attraction.

In the end, they had the intimate conviction that it would not work, and that is exactly what happened, too many expectations on the part of this power, believing that everything would come magically, arms crossed to have positive thoughts, what they lacked was the interaction with the outside world, had in their subconscious only thoughts of need and deprivation, invoking vain hopes.

Fortunately for you, and thanks to this book, you will have the secret of a happy and successful life, and this for free (apart from the price of the book, this is obvious, which is not excessive either).

Our universe is governed by a natural magnetism, with a positive and negative polarity, just as there is a North Pole and a South Pole. If you take a magnet and rub it with a sewing needle and put it on a cork, placed in a bowl of water, it will show you the north, most have already experienced it in physics class when you were at school.

Each element that constitutes our world works according to the same rules from the atomic point of view, including all the atoms that constitute our body, and our way of thinking, seeing the world and considering events have a natural magnetism.

All this creates harmony with the universe, some elements are attracted to each other, while others repel, either in the visible or in the invisible, physical or spiritual.

Our way of thinking creates magnetism in the

form of an aura that can be beneficial or harmful, and emerges in each one of us, attracting or repelling according to the dominant traits.

As a result, your inner world is a reflection of your outer world, whether in the way we view your environment, how we feel about it, and the interactions we have with other individuals.

By reconsidering many of your positive thoughts, the positive will come to you. When you think about abundance, that is, when you feel that you have nothing to lack and everything is at your disposal, you are happy with what you have, and it extends outside of yourself. Your current life, which you see as poor, will remain poor until you reconsider your universe.

Your expectations and wishes will come true if you start to appreciate what you already have, the most important thing, life, the power to act, interact, see, listen, counteract a landscape is the most beautiful treasure, the world itself is a wealth.

Live the present moment with the firm conviction that we can achieve it, although nothing around us predisposes us to it. It is about changing the mood and conceiving external events as passengers. The sun is always behind the clouds. Basically, you need to relativize everything that is happening in your life in a positive way. Everything that has been said in your youth and in your life, you must learn from it. For example, to tell yourself that this individual who has been very hard with you has only made you stronger, hardened you, and it is from this wealth that you must draw, from your ability to receive the blows, not to fatalize about the situation of your existence, as proof, you read to me, it means that in you, there is an inestimable reserve that you want to exploit.

Take a fixed point you want to reach, it is your goal, and in your heart, you must remain convinced of achieving it at all costs, no matter how long it takes you, nothing should deviate from your goal, the road to success.

Through this, it is necessary to project a dynamic vision of your thoughts, to go in the direction of concretion. That is, use your imagination (your inner world) to move it to the real world (the outside world), and this, from now on, without postponing, even a draft, a few words on a piece of paper ... But you lack the essential, the "*information*", for that, everything is at your disposal here and now, here and now, on the Internet, in television documentaries, in books, always in search of elements, of material to work .

And above all, never tell yourself that we know enough until the goal is reached (and even after), we never learn enough.

Changes in your life, in your appearance, will not be visible at the beginning, and gradually, by small external signs, you will see that you are on the right path.

As for the "*cyclicals*" as I explained in my first book, we all depend on two cycles, one positive and one negative, and as a result, we live in the same world, but with a different perception of it.

The environment will respond by resonance with what we are, that is, if you think negatively, external events will also be, by your words, your thoughts and your attitude towards life in general, you believe that you are not capable of doing something, even if you try, the psychological response will be that you will be incapable of acting, you will be clumsy, untrained, then you will surrender. If you think that everyone is angry with you, it will appear in relation to your behavior and facial features, we will tend to flee from you. Besides that, you will have a negative aura, the one you have made.

Even if you change your behavior, it will take some time, because we can not interrupt the current cycles, but mitigate its effects by making the positive cycle grow, this can not be done directly, because until the revolution (or cycle) is completed, it will not happen nothing, and the next one will still have negative aspects, but it will be reduced, you will feel the effects over time.

Do not think more in terms of "*lack*", but of "*gain*", feel that you have everything in your power, appreciate everything that life offers you, the power to see, hear, touch, all the treasures that you neglect, because too focused on the "*need*". Assume you have everything you need to be happy, it will look in your face and you will have better relationships. Do you want to get more? This must be done by working on yourself and for others, what do you want to contribute to the world? Everything is already at your disposal, to be willing to act in the collective interest, not to ask, but to give, time, money, listen or help. As Max Piccinini would say: "To change your outer world, you have to change your inner world!"

Tell yourself: "*Yes, I can do it! I have all the means to do it!*"

If you do exactly what I have told you, your life will be different, it will not be visible now, but if you compare it with a year ago, you will say "*wow!*", But I warn you that the process will be a little long depending on your willingness to act, so I insist, start right now!

Reshaping the subconscious mind

It is possible to reshape your subconscious, change the interpretation of our thoughts in front of a past event, in fact, in my opinion, it would be necessary to put in perspective, for example, that there is free evil and that for yourself, you know exactly what you are worth , in this particular case, you will have to prove what you really are worth, go beyond all pretensions and judgments.

To do this, you would have to convince yourself, reinterpret your thoughts by creating new neuro-associated connections, I insist on this point throughout this book, because I believe it is an important part of subjective reprogramming.

The memories of your life are within you, even if you can not remember them, the stimuli of these previous events remain in you. The subconscious is as agitated as *Nicolas Sarkozy* for having drunk too much coffee (for the foreigners, if the book will be translated, it is a French head of state known for his nervousness).

At some point in your life, what happened in your childhood or even after will reappear in the form of these same stimuli.

For example, if a friend offers to raise you or you have to climb a ladder, you answer that you are not interested, but you do not know why.

Actually, your subconscious mind responds in your place, makes the connection between this information and the events of the past, being younger, you have fallen precisely from a ladder, a safety mechanism has been activated, or perhaps you have been overprotected, or even called incapable.

The action presented will be associated to an

earlier memory that at first glance does not have a dazzling memory, but the associated emotion is very present.

As you grow older and in the form of a "*vice repetitas*," your first thoughts created suspicions, and the more you evolve in life, and the more the sign grew, the more it was as if you were turning on the "*Volume*" button on your radio

.

This explains, in large part, the shyness and lack of confidence, your conscience (through your subconscious), has put yourself in a "*self-protection*" mode, will consider that if you do an action, you will have a negative reaction, it will look identical what you have known, and deep down, why would it change?

So it's easy for you to give up, tell yourself: "*What's the point of trying?*" And it is at that precise moment when you agree with all those people who have judged you negatively, you will continue being "*a loser*", "*a useless*" .

To reverse the trend, we must follow the same path in the opposite direction, create new "*vice repetitas*" by obscuring the old cognitive data, because they remain dominant and their unconscious can silence their dominant emotions, as well as the perceptions related to this new information, our brain is marvelous in its power of remodeling, to create new paths of access the area to condition it, said this will not happen overnight, because it has already needed to be given form to all its current existence.

The process of remodeling can only be done by the force of habit, it is like inserting a foreign body into our body, when implanting it, the immune mechanism will be activated creating rejection of it, for the body to assimilate it, it will take time and patience, and if it is not, it must become it.

Take control and listen only to yourself, envy those who succeed and want to do the same? Then go ahead! Try it! Try it! You will be surprised by the result, but first of all, you need to work on your self-confidence. How do you do it? Simply by training, the search for new information that reading can provide, for example, will give you confidence in your thoughts, your subconscious feeds on it.

And above all, stop believing that everything will happen as if by magic, as I mentioned in my first book on personal investment, we have nothing for nothing! If there is true magic, it would come from your will! For this purpose, I recommend that you feed your subconscious mind with positive thoughts! How? Through works related to this field, in particular those of *Norman Vincent Peal, Franck Nicolas, Max Piccinini, or Napoleon Hill.* Summarize all your reading, and everything will seem obvious if you not only read, but also understand and feel curious, this is the key to your success.

Perception of wealth and poverty

What would happen if you did not have anyone by your side?

Is there no possibility of interactions with a retinue? In this particular case, one could imagine someone living in the desert as a hermit who only lives on himself, searching for water miles from his house on foot, and hunting as much as he can.

Few people have this capacity, victims of what could be called "*the consumer society*", we no longer hunt and we no longer collect water kilometers away, all you have to do is take your car and buy at the local supermarket, so we have become dependent on this system.

However, we still know how to make a difference, thanks to our work, we are at the service of as many people as possible indirectly, for example, when I worked a long time ago in the supermarket distribution sector, I put on the shelves products that were going to be sold to their customers, which gave me an income.

Among the consumers were the owners of garages, the ironmongers and all kinds of people with whom I had interacted at least once, thanks to the fruit of my work coming from a service rendered, they in turn did me a favor, repairing my car, selling me nails and screws for a cabinet I was making.

The point of union between both is money, a means of exchange that has replaced what was done in distant times, barter, the exchange of one service for another, the digger of wells gave water for bread to the baker, the horticulturist he changed his crops for meat to the hunter, etc ...

Each one brought something to the greatest number in exchange for another good, each at the service of the collective interest.

What does this period of history have in common with the present? If I take the baker, for example, he "*owns*", that is, he can satisfy a need in the community, his bakery has a lot of bread, and thanks to the money he gets from the product he sells, he can buy more to make, but also to pay to his employees and to support yourself. Thus, at the time of the meal, the baker "*always*" has bread from his bakery, wine from the vine grower, fruit and vegetables from the gardener and, above all, the energy to work and gain strength to return to work.

In all areas of daily life, we serve the community directly and indirectly in exchange for a good or service, either as an employer or as an employee, it is the fruit of our work that enriches us, whether in the manufacture of self parts, in supermarkets, in masonry, and the more we serve the interest of the greater number, the more we enrich ourselves.

Some people are proud of their work, of what they have, believing that they have everything they need, and there are others, jealous of those who have everything and are richer. But when we are not satisfied with what we have, we are unhappy.

Looking at things from a new perspective, we always have what we need, whether in money or in goods and services, whatever form it takes, it is still something that exists in the material world.

For this, most people who do not carelessly get the greatest treasure they possess, the "*spirit*".

It is by the way we think from our subconscious that wealth or poverty is produced, by the way we interpret events, and it is also what determines our destiny, the way we look at the outside world.

For example, the word "*treasure*" can mean a chest full of gold coins, or the fruit of your labor, or nature, but it can mean health, there are so many ways that one could give a "*treasure*".

Most people are poor, because deep down they feel poor, there we can also give several meanings to this term, "*poverty of spirit*", "*economic poverty*", or "*poverty in relationships*", they feel that they do not They have nothing because they have not perceived the "*treasure*" they have in them.

If I ask you what it means to you to be "*rich*", what would be the first thought you have? Of course, I anticipate your answer, knowing the human mind, you will tend to align yourself with what I have just told you, in which case, I congratulate you, because you assimilate the founding principle of the subconscious mind.

Indeed, some would think that to be rich is to own 1 million euros, they say to themselves "*if I were rich, I would buy a house, a sports car, etc ...*". Therefore, they are waiting and feeling poor because they do not have, deep down in their hearts this feeling of" *lack* "is created (I will often return to it), they are conditioned to poverty, whereas if the thoughts are oriented towards real wealth, health, nature, the goods we possess (even the old ones), create the conditions that lead us to success, the dominant feeling in their minds is abundance, this gives them a feeling of sufficiency, and they live happy

And there is much more, because they contribute time and energy to others, what they receive in return is gratitude, love or joy.

I can tell you this, for those who believe me, you are already very rich, look around you, what do you see? Relations? Modern equipment? Do you have money in your wallet? Do you have a roof over your head? Therefore, keep in mind that "you own, therefore, you are rich".

And I would like to make a correction in the way you perceive the money, it will probably surprise some people, but getting rich is giving, and getting poorer is asking, is not it strange?

That's why most of them do not evolve, because they have a reverse perception of money, which, I remind you, did not exist at some point in history. Nor does he have the concept of value, because, for example, if he owns an old car, align his thoughts on the collective opinion, saying that it is archaic, that it is a matter of shipwreck, that it provokes in his heart this feeling of impoverishment, listening to others, you would see the functional side, the utility, a means of locomotion that would guide you from point A to point B. It is an asset, an advantage of your efforts, something you have, while others do not.

The human mind often tends to look up instead of down. Envy those who go to luxury restaurants or drive beautiful cars, who have millions of euros, you want to be like them, when in essence you already are, what you look at is the way, In terms of aspects of your life and comparing them with yours, there is that feeling of jealousy in you, this need to be in that high level of existence, and what happens if I tell you that you can?

Money, luxury and everything that revolves around it are only technical aspects, and you compare them with your life that you consider miserable, whereas if you look below you, there are individuals who do not possess what you have, you are more rich that they, and everything you own only has the value you give (I'll also return about it)

Let me give you an example ... Take a pen, look! How much do you think it's worth? 0.50 €? Now, imagine that you have in your hand the pen that *Justin Bieber* used to write his last song and sign autographs. I can guarantee that you would give much more in terms of value, maybe 50,000 euros to more than 10 million euros. Why? Because you value things as you value them and that is what happens in an auction, if the *Leonardo Da Vinci* had not painted the Jonconde, or if it were not famous, it would only be A canvas like so many others, with their similarities, painting, canvas , frames, wood, varnish, etc ...?

If you all have a television at home, consider it as a good, what you have earned, what is in your possession, and the value to give it is the result of your work, used every day to watch series or movies.

Another reason why you think you are poor is the little consideration of the value of something of nature, which you can find everywhere, in the forest, in the mountains or by the sea.

To be rich in your outer world, you have to be rich in your inner world, either in the way you feel prosperous or in the way you consider the value of the things you find in your life.

To get to the beginning of this game, if you were alone, with whom would you count? In person except yourself! Do not wait for someone to help you and help you stay, do you want to drink? Then, go for miles to find water! are you hungry? Then hunt! Do not wait until it rains or the rabbit you want to eat sounds at the door with its small legs.

Most people do not manage because they trust too much in others and expect too much from life, they say, they want ...... They need ...., jealous of those who succeed, while They do not draw from their own treasure, they covet those of others.

Reestimate your value, and you will see, you will quickly become a millionaire, in a 15 €

chair, estimate that it is worth 50 €, or even 100 €, but in the end, the real value is in each one of us, and that is what we have to offer what makes us rich, that has nothing to offer and that says to be poor.

I hope you begin to understand the nuance and that your perception changes in money, think in this way and your life will be more bearable, put your life in perspective, it is already very rich.

The notions of pain and pleasure

We all have dreams that we would like to come true, but how do we fulfill them?

I was like you for a long time, and life has taught me that the most important thing is to be satisfied with what you already have, to learn to appreciate what you have. Look outside your house, you see people who have very little, who would like to have what you have, a roof over your head, a TV and all modern conveniences.

But deep down, we want more and more, faced with the obsolescence of the equipment we have, an argument used by the manufacturers of mobile phones or household appliances.

And of course, we fall into the trap.

So what does the notion of pain and pleasure mean? it is simply the fact of being satisfied with what you have even if you want everything and immediately, what many people usually do, but through that, if you spend your money on more modern equipment, without waiting, it will be morally painful not to have the means to offer you the vacation of your dreams, for example, all this because you wanted to offer a more modern equipment and rebuild your home.

Without pain, there is no pleasure and conversely, it is about making great sacrifices to get what you want, set aside, work harder, invest deeply telling yourself that in the end a beautiful reward awaits you, even if the first results are unsatisfactory. Do not stop trying!

To go further

Do you know the theory of Ping-pong ball? Do not? Of course, I just invented it. (created by the author for this book).

To do this, imagine a glass of water half full, it represents the world in which you live! The liquid corresponds to poverty in general and the air in the glass symbolizes wealth. It is about two different environments.

So imagine a ping-pong ball, it's about you, the shell represents your carnal envelope, and inside is the air or the water, it's your inner environment, your world, your way of thinking.

If the ball is full of water, it will remain at the bottom of the cup in a water environment, but if it is full of air, it will float in an air environment.

This phenomenon is universal, the inner world corresponds to the outside world, its external environment will always reflect what they think, and yet the liquid in the glass does not change, the ball does not change, it is only what happens inside what varies.

Theory of the Ping-pong ball

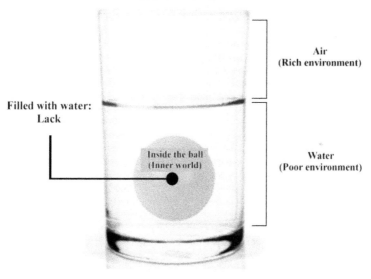

Glass of water
(Outside world)

Air
(Rich environment)

Filled with water:
Lack

Inside the ball
(Inner world)

Water
(Poor environment)

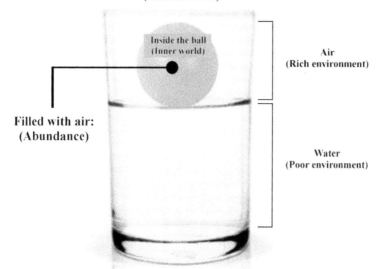

Glass of water
(Outside world)

Inside the ball
(Inner world)

Air
(Rich environment)

Filled with air:
(Abundance)

Water
(Poor environment)

The exterior reflects the interior

According to the theory I just mentioned, the ping-pong ball represents your bubble, and inside is the perception that you have of your outer world, it is in perfect harmony with what you think and feel. The ball does not put up any resistance and will always be in the same environment. If there is air inside, the outside will be the same.

Therefore, for the law of attractiveness for work, you have to remain authentic. What is happening, and why you are not evolving, immersed in the same environment, is that deep down you do not believe in it, even if you all give yourself the means to achieve it. On the one hand, you create the external conditions by creating your own business for example, and on the other hand, your subconscious and always oriented towards need, the desire to succeed and be rich. This retains all its authenticity.

If you are in need or waiting for something, a result or a profit of money, you are similar to a poor person who asks for alms to the universe, the signal that you send to everything that surrounds you is that you do not have. We could compare it with human interactions, each individual you know in your life is just a reflection of yourself, the way you perceive and behave with them. What you release within you is felt by those around you. Around him is his vibratory bubble that sends a signal to his surroundings.

The problem is double, on the one hand, by wanting to place yourself above others, you see them poorer than you, you see them waiting for the satisfaction of a need that you would like to satisfy. On the other hand, you have the same need when you want to sell, but nobody can buy you anything, because you see them poor, even though you feel that the bank does not have the financial means to help you perceive it in the same way. Actually, you want to sell what you do not have to people who do not have anything. In this case, your interior reflects the exterior.

To optimize your chances of success, you must think differently, not in terms of needs or expectations, see others and your environment as your own reflection, see the unsuspected wealth of each of the people you know, without seeing their conditions social or your bank account, see only the human, and everyone can give to others. Look at all the riches of this world, what nature can give you, what you have thanks to it, life, health, the pleasure of looking at beautiful landscapes, that's what a real treasure is, we all have it in each one of us.

Relearn again what it means to be rich, and you will be surprised at what will happen in your life. However, do not try to deceive your subconscious mind, which only accepts what is authentic. You will not cheat a bank with a false check you have made, because your subconscious is the same, your imagination will not be enough to change your social status without perceiving the outside world with a different eye, and without recognizing in the bottom that you are already very rich, it is not enough to think like that, you must have the intimate conviction, and you work on it.

How to enrich your mind?

Through training. Your subconscious mind is already conditioned by the life you lead, having little knowledge, you will discover treasures in the books. Many authors will bring you another philosophy of life, to see otherwise, it will not be enough to read, but to invest 100%, submerge, immerse yourself, be in the head of the author, of those who have been successful, you will have your point of view on the world.

On the other hand, if you are not interested in reading, it would mean that you are not interested in the universe of the great thinkers of this world, however, he is one of the most successful people of his time and one that inspired others afterwards. Through the fruit of knowledge, you will have, through instruction, much to offer yourself and others, you can also share. The power of knowledge is magical, it opens doors that even you could not have crossed through lack of confidence and knowledge.

In addition, your subconscious will accept this new authentic information, it will be part of yourself, you are not inventing it, because it comes from the outside world. Get used to thinking that you already have everything at your disposal to be rich. Stay focused on abundance and not lack. Do not look at what is happening, do not covet, do not get jealous, everything you need, you already have it, it's up to you to know how to use it enjoying what you already have!

CHAPTER 6: THE EXTERNAL DOMI-NATION OF THE SUBCONSCIOUS MIND

"First we must build a society, where the personal act finds a greater value than the manufacture of things and the manipulation of beings. »
(Ivan Illich)

Is it possible to dominate the subconscious mind?

My clear answer is yes, to prove it, there are already proven practices called brainwashing.

You have been victims of it from an early age because of the adults and friendships that have influenced, or even modified, your belief systems to the point that it is part of you.

How does the system work? The subject is isolated, in the grip of new ideas that are constantly being hammered. This principle was already seen during the Second World War with the youth of Hitler, or more recently with terrorists who use techniques of indoctrination and mental conditioning to induce subjects to commit morally challenging acts.

When the individual is young, he is in the discovery phase, assimilating something to pain or pleasure, and this is best recorded in the subconscious.

For adults, it is not impossible either, but the disinvestment phase is easier to undo, simply recovering the old belief system.

Recently, I had the opportunity to read Anthony Robbins' book *"The Awakening of Power Within."* Inside, the author evokes partisan manipulations of the Korean War, forcing hundreds of Americans to federate with the communist regime and indirectly betraying their country, and signing documents that praise the benefits of communism. . For their relatives and officers, they were fervent American patriots, what led them to join the enemy camp and its ideologies?

Koreans have used a fairly efficient technique that I would call *"voluntary submission"* (technique still used today).

The subject is locked in a cell, and his captors visit him regularly, not to torture him, but to obtain news, offer him cigarettes, alcohol, food and magazines that promote the merits of the communist regime, provide him with many propaganda tools and argue with him in friend-ly terms.

By winning capital of sympathy, without forc-ing to extort information, the subject gives them of himself and indirectly during simple conversations, becoming more comfortable with the enemy. It's a very long process, but it's worth it for its effectiveness. What is hap-pening is a form of adaptability of the sur-rounding environment. With time, the prisoner gets used to the walls, he only sees that around him, as well as the Koreans who seem likeable at first sight.

This same technique strongly pushes Catholics to become extremist Muslims, demonstrating the fragility of the human spirit, which remains very malleable for some.

Conscious and unconscious hypnosis

There is a difference between the two phases of mind control, first of all the direct transmis-sion of suggestions in the waking state, and the other in a state of deep sleep. The uses are ve-ry varied, there is first of all the one that contributes to the well-being, it is the therapeu-tic hypnosis whose medicine begins to open its doors, it is a subjective healing, very useful for the individuals suffering in particular from hypochondria. Psychologists practice methods related to hypnosis, inviting the patient to sleep. When they enter it (the subconscious), and with the help of the information provided by the patient, they detect the elements that cause the disorders of their daily life.

Added to this is therapeutic self hypnosis, which consists of convincing oneself (self-conviction), whether in the waking or sleep state.

These two forms (and others), include suggestions in the subconscious, then use them in the unconscious to make combinations with the information collected, to create new neuro-associations that will modify the value fields.

There is also the hypnosis of the world of entertainment that only serves to distract the public, either in a room or on the street. The suggestions can be made consciously, that is, the spectator does not even realize that he has been hypnotized, so we see him giving without realizing it, signing a document, giving the impression of being absent, lost in thought, answering directly to the suggestions of the hypnotist. The interaction can also be passive, that is, the viewer is in a phase of deep sleep, we can see his body harden like a steel beam, and bear the weight of fifteen people on it.

Then, and finally, there is hypnosis for specific purposes, used in phases of espionage or indoctrination.

Experiments have been conducted with young individuals. They had to put the headphones on their ears before falling asleep. The tape they were going to hear had a blank space of about 30 minutes, which was expected to be waiting for a deep sleep.

Before they had done resistance exercises to tire the body, reading exercises and concentration until they felt tired. They were locked in a soundproof white room, inside which was a condor-type armchair (foam chair for relaxation, still available in the market).

In the first place, they were in a state of relaxation, the young people had to relax their bodies, put on their headphones and let themselves be submerged in a state of deep sleep.

Subliminal suggestions accompanied by soft music that cradled the participants were written on the magnetic tape. At the end of the session, the tape suggested that they wake up, and without realizing it, they had recorded new information, then they had to answer a series of questions, and the results were surprising, 85% of them were able to answer all the questions correctly, just 15% of the remaining group, or could not finish it, or answered only a few questions.

This shows the power of the unconscious. Edgar Cayces is an example. This man knew nothing about medicine, but in his youth, and under hypnosis, he was able to give accurate diagnoses and appropriate treatments to people with disorders that even certified doctors could not treat or even understand the symptoms.

Hypnosis can work in two ways, in a state of deep and awake sleep, and can be used for therapeutic purposes or to obtain information.

There was also what I would call hypnosis of the show, in France (also to address the foreign public), there was a hypnosis show, the guests were under the influence of a hypnotist named *Mesmer*.

They were in unlikely situations, like participating in a television show called "*The Bachelor*" where one of them had to marry a pony, another that he thought was a vampire, and another that he really thought was in a cockpit while he was in a flight simulator ... The debate is still open, although the chain that issues this program defends itself of all deception, the doubt is still allowed and everyone keeps their own opinion. Mesmer's technique is called "*conscious hypnosis*", the subject is not directly in a state of deep sleep, the hypnotist has priority over the consciousness to master it, with one hand diverts his attention before putting it to sleep, then communicates directly with the subconscious giving instructions. We speak then of receptivity, that is to say, that consciousness lets information pass, unlike those that are not receptive, still resistance, like *Gandalf* (Lord of the Rings character), from the top of his mountain and brandishing his staff shouting "you will not pass!"

Personally, I believe in it, others are free to validate or not the power of conscious hypnosis. For the rest, the Mesmer case remains a mystery. The control of the human mind has existed since the dawn of time, but hypnosis experienced its golden age towards the end of the 19th century. However, I will mention a period in which it has already been used many times.

During the Cold War, Russia and the United States suspected each other, agents were recruited to find out a little more about the other's intentions by spying on them. To ensure that none of them revealed information that was useful to the enemy, for some were hypnotized, the details of their lives fell asleep, while creating a new identity, these agents (Russians and Americans) were convinced that they were on the side of the enemy, so when one of them was captured, and had to pass a lie detector, no information was revealed about their real lives.

In another equally disturbing case, in Russia, a hypnotist had managed to elude all the surveillance systems of the Kremlin, had managed to pass without problems to the escort of Stalin until it was close enough to him. Stalin, fearful of his safety, ordered that he be put in jail. Previously, this individual had managed to obtain a significant amount of money from a bank of the cashier, using a simple white paper, which appeared as an official document in the mind of the person who was going to give him a briefcase full of notes. The hypnotist, once he was gone, left his simple sheet of blank paper to the cashier, who soon realized the deception. Fortunately for him, the experiment was aimed at a documentary about hypnosis, the money was returned to the bank without too many problems.

Principle of the sponge

To describe the process, take a sponge, and immerse it in a container of water dyed red, if we
do this for several years, it will turn all red, it
will have taken the color of water.

If we take this same sponge, and submerge it
in a basin dyed blue, the red pigments that are
impregnated, even a thousand times, will remain red, and over time, repeating the operation for several years, it will start to turn pur-
ple, the red color that will be impregnated for
a long time.

Now, suppose there is the possibility of remov-
ing the red pigments, putting them in a container of clear water, before submerging them in
a container of blue water, the first dye will
fade with time, giving way to a magnificent
blue tint.

Phases of beliefs, fears and indoctrination

Fear is a good tool for propaganda, leaving no
choice but to comply with the demands of the
dominant, or we adhere or suffer, which is reduced to "*get under duress*."

This technique is used by terrorists, among others, but their messages are also transmitted by the media. I do not mean newspapers or television news; in these cases, they would be accomplices in the distribution of their propaganda, although the media operate differently to transmit these messages, through the Internet, among other means.

Speaking of the media, some (whom I can not name) use methods to get a candidate elected in presidential elections, pressing as much as possible to bring information to our subconscious, practice a form of "*vice repetitas*" ", the information is that it is repeated regularly on television, radio, newspapers and the Internet.

If we take the name of *Jean-Manuel Macrochon*, candidate of "*La France en Marche*", for example, his name will be repeated more than 20,000 times in just two days, a form of unconscious suggestion, the television program will be adapted to create connections neuronal, representing a hairy candidate, making his rival, the candidate of "*La République en chemise*", *Florent Fabiozy*, pale, whose armor on his crown would delight the hairdressers. The advantage of the latter is that it does not have a single white hair.

The method of repetition is also used by advertisers, who make a striking slogan, but also by mentalists, experts in mental manipulation. They are based on the behavior of the body, without the human mind having secrets for them.

The mnemonic, bringing his reference point back to the choice of a color for example, red, there is on the stage, a fire extinguisher, a tomato, a STOP panel and many other objects of this color, which have been voluntarily placed so that your attention is focused on them. As a result, the mentalist does not read your mind, but unconsciously directs it, you only have to see where your eyes are (necessarily a red object), and it says "*I bet you have chosen this color*!", You answer stunned " *how did you do it?* "(note that the part is also red). The only thing that could deceive a mentalist in this case is that you are color blind from birth, so there is no visual reference point.

The field of synthesis, which consists of the mentalist asking you the preliminary questions related to this color, indirectly, will condition you. For example, you will start talking about the firefighters in this interview with you, tell you anecdotes about this color (red), indirectly, your mind will assimilate it, the point of origin analyzing this information in relation to what you already know.

The danger of sects and other organizations

Personally, I'm not asking you to adhere to all my beliefs, I'm just talking about a topic in my book, a very specific topic, and the information I have. I refer, of course, to sects and other similar organizations.

It is possible to manipulate individuals en masse, and for the weakest in mind to be guided by fear and lack.

For example, if someone encounters difficulties in life, it leaves fertile ground for him to easily manipulate his mind.

In fact, what is the average individual looking for? Security and money, he would like to see his problems disappear, always harassed by creditors, without finding the means to solve his difficulties, and also have the financial consolation to protect him and his family.

You must be aware that this type of individuals belong to a sphere that you will never reach, except by your own means and using your head. They use your mental weakness, they play with your hopes for a better life, when only you can decide what you want.

CHAPTER 7: EXCEED YOUR LOSS OF CONFIDENCE

"Creativity is such a delicate flower that, although compliments make it flourish, discouragement can prevent it from flourishing. »
(Alex Osborn)

Self-confidence

What you are inside yourself, is outside, is a universal truth that can be found in books like the Bible that should be interpreted as a collection of truths.

If you have a very negative perception of life, you have to redirect it towards the positive, you are capable of doing it, others have been before you, and others will be after you.

Think of all those who have succeeded brilliantly in their careers, it has not been by chance, because they have come to believe in themselves that they can do it.

How does the system work? Look around you, your family, your friends, why do they perceive you in one way and not another? Because depending on how you behave with others also determines how they will react to you, it is the principle of cause and effect.

But beware, to improve your outer world, you must first do it within yourself, perceive the events in a positive way, what I call the process of "*self-conviction*".

You must see with a new eye everything that has clouded your life, form another conditioning of your subconscious, draw strength from the weaknesses, chase away the "great Lulu" that destroyed you, as well as all the others who have degraded you. You are the only captain of your ship invaded by mutineers, who are no more than the bad thoughts acquired by others, throw them overboard and continue sailing alone.

When you see people who do not listen to you, who tend to depreciate or exploit you, move them away! They only slow down their plans, the people to avoid are the planners, the speculators, the liars and the cheaters, they are people who contaminate their mind, as far as possible, they stop thinking or go out with them and come back. At the center of your success, you and what you do to progress.

Envy and jealousy are what dominate the weak, are synonyms of lack, and in this case the majority of the human race belongs to this category that does not exploit the wealth that the world can provide.

What if I told you that you are already very rich? I can tell you this, because life is a very beautiful gift that you should not neglect, although you think about its hardness, it allows us a lot of interaction with the outside world, you enjoy the world that surrounds you, the air you breathe, you discover nature and you share emotions with other people, what you can not do once you're dead, some will say *"great! They'll forget me!"* but in this case, why do you want to be successful? This means making yourself known!

Do you honestly think that Bill Gate, if he had that kind of thought, would have gotten where he is now? Of course not.

What is wrong is that you are seeing the wrong people who are very happy not to see you evolve, who turn to the right ones, to those who have education, who are socially and financially successful, and who seek help from them.

In addition, to return to what I said about wealth, they are already compared to some countries of the world, they contemplate the landscape when a blind man can not, he hears music, but for a man. Deaf, he does not know the magic of a sound and a silence can not create a radio program (for example), when he can afford it.

Most would like to have what you have, a roof over your head, a car, Internet and food, imagine that in the poorest countries, there are people who do not have access to all this.

To put things even more in perspective with everything I just said, singers like *Andrea Bocceli* and *Gilbert Montagné* became famous, but they were blind from birth, *Philippe Croizon,* whom I already mentioned in my first book, had no arms or legs and, nevertheless, he managed to cross the English Channel by swimming, and with the strength of his will, they managed to get one that no one with all his physical abilities could do.

Relativize with all this, you are capable of all your functions, visual, motor, auditory, you have an unsuspected wealth, when you understand this, you can say that you are already rich in your life.

To go beyond what life has to offer you, first

you must appreciate what we already have, when this notion enters your mind, then, everything is possible, be convinced of it!

Now say it inside you and put it in your mind! *"YES! I CAN DO IT!"*

And to conclude, convince yourself of one thing too, nothing is simple in life, but with great will, you can do anything! It will not be obvious at first, but you should not stop at failures, it is precisely the basis of your success, and it shows that you have tried, while others spend their lives ruminating that they will not succeed! In this particular case, imagine the number of potential talents that have fallen into oblivion, are buried in the mind of its creator, like his physical body, locked in a fir box.

Coca Cola, the first year of its creation, was not a resounding success. This company, which has only sold about twenty bottles, has become a very large group that sells its drinks worldwide and weighs billions.

If you have this deep conviction in you, you will be surprised at what you could achieve. Act from the bottom of your heart and your whole being, be driven by this impulse of success, believe in yourself and change your perception of the world around you.

Failure is a lesson in life

We all face during our lives the failures that lead us to surrender from the first attempt. Even if you try several times, you find yourself facing a wall, as if something is not working, and you get the feeling that nothing is possible, even for future projects.

So remember this, when we try, it's because we want to improve, but when failures are too frequent, at some point in our lives, we give up, and we think, why bother again?

And this program you to stay in your comfort zone, believing that everything you have undertaken for a long time was doomed to failure, this state seems permanent but nothing is frozen in time. What's going on? Why do you always fail? Because deep down, that is what will inevitably happen. It is important that you remember this, what you are inside will be reflected out. Even if external circumstances do not allow it, you are permanently convinced in the background, and in spite of the failed attempts, you will succeed!

This will not happen in a day, in fact, you are

dragged into a cycle that, whatever happens, will lead to failure, I do not want to scare or discourage you by saying that, but I'm just saying that not everything will happen the next day.

If nothing happens after one year, do not worry! Tell yourself that the spiral you are in is shrinking, only that you should not give up or let the old habits dominate, as you begin, you will also initiate a new cycle oriented towards the positive, whose circumstances will bring about a new spiral that will grow through a phenomenon of cause and effect, and reduce the impact of the negative universe that you have created for yourself. Never be in a hurry to get results, as this puts you in a fault pattern. Just do the best you can every day to improve your situation, it will be difficult, I know, but the most important thing is to always believe in it, to have faith. Create the cause, and you will get the effect!

What I would recommend is that you start now without finding excuses, it is the weak who have excuses, not the people who want to strengthen themselves internally.

You will not be able to replace twenty years of misfortunes and failures at one time, in the best of cases, it will take you a full year to three years, in the worst case, it can take years, but in any case, even if you do not have the desired life the first year, you will feel the impacts in your daily life, you will notice the changes in your environment, they will be small signals, attention that they will give you, even the people with whom you have not had contact for a long time, will come back to you, ¿ why? because everything you bring to the universe will have started to work. As soon as you see the first signs, it will mean you are on the right track, so when this happens, do not let go and move on, do not let the fatality you created in your life overpower you!

The strength of habits

If you put yourself to work every day, no matter how much time you spend on it, it will become your habit, your subconscious will better accept the changes over time.

Everyone tends to give up after a few days, simply because you are in the grip of your old habits.

For a young beginner in the professional world, he is always supervised by a trainer who explains how his job works, and for someone who does his job well, lets him try it, why?

If the young person only takes notes, he can learn them by heart, but he has no idea with which to associate them, there will be no visual, tactile or auditory reference, the memory works with the five senses, if he does not see the object, it can be an elevator, a computer or a transport vehicle, if the theory is not accompanied by practice, it would be like a summer without sun, *Emmanuel Macron* without *Brigitte*, *Donald Trump* without *Mc Donalds* or *François Hollande* without charisma ... (Forget this last example ... !!).

Just so you know that reading the summary of a book does not tell you the whole story, and I'm even convinced that most of you who have seen my book and have not read it will not get all the benefits, they'll say the subject is interesting without knowing the details and the little secrets, including the one they told me some time ago in the *Chamonix casino*.

In the case of our young man, take notes and say: "*It's okay, it's clear!*" It's only for the coach to leave him alone, because he does not seem very enthusiastic if he does not ask a question, the next morning he will get lost with his bad grades.

Then he will ask you questions like: "*Can you show me how to do it?*" The latter will explain everything to you during a period of 15 days to a month (if after that, the young person still does not understand anything, it is because he does not show a great interest in his work).

Your subconscious mind sends a signal to your conscience exposing your great interest or not in the subject exposed, if you are enthusiastic, you will ask questions to collect the missing information, on the other hand, if your feeling is boring, you will reject it completely, your attention it focuses elsewhere, in particular on the secretary at the photocopier who would be curious to know during the break for coffee.

In addition, the change of environment modifies the subconscious, although the old remains engraved in the consciousness, it will be stored in a very distant place in the depths of your memory and the feelings associated with it, in the depths of the subconscious.

At the beginning of his professional life, the student keeps the traces of his school environment that dominate his thoughts that dominated his whole childhood by the force of habit.

The more he adapts to his new surroundings and his habits, the more he will dominate, letting the knowledge he has acquired escape him for lack of practice.

The subconscious, a great decision-maker, no longer sees the meaning of knowing mathematics, history or French because this young individual has simply moved on to something else.

What would have allowed him to maintain all his cognitive faculties is passion, if a student does not have this fiber in him, he can not do anything (unfortunately).

Ambitions so abused

"*When I grow up, I'll be a police officer, an airplane pilot or an astronaut ....*" We all think about our future profession as children, inspired by people known as *Alain Prost* and *Michel Platini* (for those of my generation), or *Thomas Pesquet* (for the younger ones), however, our dreams were still dreams, because as we grew, these projects still seemed far away, instead of seeing that we were getting closer.

How is this possible? Our educational system would have allowed us to reach more or less our goals if we were not distracted by children's shows, video games or movies, our minds were far from education, the subconscious mind rejected a lot of useful information for our conscience, because there is a pleasure dominant, our parents are largely responsible for it, letting us see the cartoons or buying a playstation (this did not exist in my time yet). Have you ever noticed that the most successful are precisely the children of those who have succeeded on their own?

One of my ex-girlfriends when I was younger came from a family whose mother was a school teacher and whose father was a merchant, my ex-girlfriend became a school teacher and, a little later, a daycare director at only 23 years old.

How was the daily life of this family of which I was a guest? (They still had not accepted me from the working class). Every morning, the awakening was very early, the breakfast balanced, and one thing that we did, because I was invited to it, it was the blessings and the reading of a passage of the Bible, for me it was new and I thought that it came from another planet, finding this a little "*funny*". The strangest thing, because it was the first time I saw this in a family, there was no television, at least, there was only one who should know about the election of *François Mitterand* as President of the Republic, to say that he was older (we were in August of 2003). He settled in a room below, stored between old books and covered with a sheet. During the entire period in which I met my ex-girlfriend, she was only turned on once during a football game, the father being a big fan. 1h30 of operation before being covered with this sheet.

My ex-girlfriend did not really know about television, some of us would say that she lived in a cave, but that's what allowed her to devote her whole mind to education, since she knew almost nothing but as a distraction, her subconscious accepted it for habit.

We, the little men we were, dreamed of success, with celebrity, we watched movies of our favorite actors, we were just spectators .....

What if we had learned to be actors? We would have studied theater, singing, mathematics, it would have allowed us to be better educated, it would have been part of our daily life and our subconscious would have accepted it as that old friend we invited to have a snack.

Fortunately for you, as for me, we can reverse

the trend and force our subconscious a bit (if you have one), do you want to compensate? Very well, but do not lengthen it, time passes at such a pace that your conscience will tell your subconscious: «*You are too old for that!* » Dare to take the first step! That is the most important! No matter how long it takes, do not think in terms of duration and live in the present moment, do it! Stop postponing one year, two years, three years, how many years will you have when you decide? Especially if it takes ten years to get it, this same period is postponed each time.

Force your subconscious mind, put your foot in the hollow of your door! A house is always built with solid foundations, if the work is hard to build, then you will have plenty of time to rest in it, proud of the achievements. The effort to learn, to open a book, if you're not used to it, at first you'll find it boring, but if you alter your subconscious a bit, do not let it dominate you, it will have drawn your life enough, it's time to regain control .

Banish what you love and welcome what you hate!

This is part of the secret that I told you about in my first book for those who have read it.

If a large strawberry cake appears on your table next to a diet cookie, what would you choose? The last thing you would say to me, is the conscious response, which everyone could say for social conditioning, but would you eat it? Your answer will be "of course yes", it is your morality that speaks and not the subconscious mind that occasionally looks at the mass, tempts you and tries to resist you.

If we put salt on the cake, would you eat it? Your answer will be clearly "*no*", your subconscious will send you the sign of disgust, you can imagine your bitterness, and yet .... If I promised to eat it for a check of € 1000, would you do it? Your answer seems to change, your subconscious acts on the priorities, and if I ask you to do it for a month, your body will find it inedible, but your mind will ask you more, because it will get used to it, destroying your body in the process, that's what what happens with fatty foods, sweet or salty, it is not your body that wants more, it is your subconscious mind that has assimilated this data to pleasure, especially having only this type of food on hand, when you smoke, consume alcohol, or when you touch drugs, it does not relieve your body in any way, it destroys it, but the neuroassociated stimuli are in action, and assimilate these substances to pleasure.

Force the mechanism by associating alcohol, cigarettes or drugs with pain, find as many negative substitutes as possible that cause rejection, and the more you do it, the more your subconscious will get used to this new information, in a day, nothing will happen It will take at least a few months, or even a whole year to get rid of these pests.

The process can also work in the other direction, take a book you would not normally read because you find it boring or difficult to understand, accustom your subconscious to changes, and your knowledge will grow as fast as the ease and desire to continue, even if would become your own drug, addicted to reading.

Good in his body and good in his head.

On the Internet, there are many life coaches, two of the most famous are *Max Piccinini* and *Franck Nicolas*, who have written books about personal development that have recently become bestsellers (Confiance Illimitée for *Franck Nicolas* and Résussite Max for *Max Piccinini*).

They are successful, they are symbols of success, and that shows that everything is possible, because they have had a difficult journey, but they have achieved it, all this from scratch.

As already mentioned in this book, and a video by *Max Piccinini* can attest to this, recalls his childhood memories, born in a modest family and resident in Strasbourg, was in an unhealthy climate in which reigned the disputes between their parents. He wanted to start a business, and it did not work very well for him, as several attempts led to his failure. One day, his mother gave him a book by Dale Carnegie entitled "*How to make friends*". When he read it, he understood where the problem came from and he said it himself in this video entitled "my story", to change his external world, he had to change his inner world. Replacing each old belief with new ones that are always pulled up, step by step, he climbs the ladder. Currently, he is a millionaire and continues to practice as a life coach in personal development organizing seminars.

The messages they transmit on social networks in a loop, either from Max or from another person, lead to a single goal, the discovery of the "*higher self*" itself.

The common point among these coaches is that they exceed their abilities, they show us how to never give up. They practice sports and train daily, and in addition, they are constantly looking for what could push them beyond what they know. The lesson they give us is that, despite all the goals achieved, we must continue and never let ourselves go.

Their secret? A healthy lifestyle, both mentally and physically. Because it is not enough to re-direct the mind towards the positive, it is ne-cessary to maintain a constancy in the thoughts, it is not done all at once, and perse-verance is worthwhile.

Along with them, an individual who lives in what might be called "*the middle class*" would seem to have a stunted growth. Without train-ing, your brain, which is thin in knowledge and training, does what might be called a "*breakdown*."

With the tools of knowledge, you will be a little more cultivated, and physical training, you will feel better with yourself and your complexes will diminish, a big step will be ta-ken and you will only have to gain confidence in yourself over time, it will come naturally, and if you make violence towards yourself, imposing a daily rhythm, it will enter into your pattern of behavior and that unconsciously.

A professional weightlifting always starts with small weights to prepare your muscles to lift more and more weight. He wants to be the best and always improve, but he is aware that to reach this level one has to go little by little.

A person who wants to put on bodybuilding just to imitate his classmates or impress his girlfriend, will "collapse", lifting 25 kg of weight without preparation and with difficulty.

Of course, there are people above you, but what is the reason for your success, for wanting everything and right now? No, through hard work, they started at the bottom of the ladder for the most part, unpretentious, evolved in life gradually, beginning with what was accessible to them, then, little by little, they continued to grow. Above all, you have to adapt before you can progress.

You will condition your body to accept ever heavier burdens, and it is the same journey as the literary culture, there is no shame in starting at the bottom, our body and our mind need to get used to the new regime, and all this by force of habit.

Fighting against the desire to surrender

Either for this book or for the first, many times I felt that I was going to give up, without thinking that I was going in the right direction, but I committed myself firmly to finish it at all costs. The proof is here, in your hands.

There is a little imp in each of us that encourages us to surrender easily, there are days when I did not feel able to continue, and yet I did.

So many times, we are absorbed by the spiral of abandonment (remember the "*cycles*" of which I spoke in my first book!), You are dragged into a series of events that drag you down, you hear that little voice in you that whispers to you "*There's no point in continuing, come on! Come with me to my world of failures!* "

When the current seems strong, you need to paddle farther away from this spiral and reach the continent that symbolizes your success.

Always go ahead despite everything, even when you have doubts or are discouraged. Keep going anyway! With little things, when the inspiration is over, tell yourself that you have a contract to honor yourself, force and force your subconscious to accept the contract, it will be difficult at first, but if you look at your project as a goal to achieve , will have the tools to build the bridge to success.

Success does not depend on the length of the step, it is still the step, build your bridge and move forward, no matter how big the stones are to build it, they are equally important.

The force of habit will enter you, it will be painful, I know, but it is the price of success, and in the end, what a beautiful reward you will have acquired.

Patience and perseverance will help you carry out your projects successfully, do not skip steps, go calmly with confidence and determination.

The syndrome of the blank page

As I write these lines, I feel overwhelmed by a multitude of thoughts and miss the inspiration. I am a victim of what is called the white page syndrome.

Of course, I do not deviate from my goals, continuing in spite of everything, and this allows me to express myself on the subject, and it can be interesting to talk about it.

My mind seems stuck in the worries of the moment, and I try to ignore them. Currently, a thousand and one thoughts are going through my mind and I have trouble keeping focused.

In my first book, I mentioned the importance of turning weaknesses into strengths and inspiring me in the elements we have. I can say that this situation falls well named (surprising?)

When this happens to you, it is normal to have moments of doubt, but the most important thing is that you take charge of your life as soon as possible.

Keep the course in your projects, this must be your driving force, your source of motivation, the effort and the reward that will come next. I promise not to give up, in this sense, to resume the cruise rhythm is essential.

I tell you why I am in such a situation, a week ago, I made a short stay in Cannes with my partner, to enjoy the beautiful summer days. This break was necessary, working more than 12 hours a day in my projects, my partner asked me to take a break to put my ideas in place, it was nice, letting me rocking for the emotions of the moment, we could stay there for years, Time stops and we enjoy the moment. But the recovery was difficult, reality is reaching us and we have to go back to work, that's everyone's business.

That's why I support the interest of working daily, so that the brain keeps pace and gets used to it, you have to make yourself violence, as if you were riding a bicycle after a fall. If I can advise you on that, always keep a fixed point, that's your goal, and no matter how you get the result, it's still the result.

PART 2: COUNSELING AND REPROGRAMMING EXERCISES

CHAPTER 8: REPROGRAMMING TIPS

"It is at a time when we least expect that life offers us a challenge to test our courage and our willingness to change, so it is useless to pretend that nothing is happening or slip away saying we are not ready yet. "
(Paulo Coelho)

What are the first steps to reprogram the sub-conscious mind?

In the first place, and to become the person you have always wanted to be and change your environment, for this you will have to break with many of your friendships that you consider toxic for you, this information, I can not give you this information, only you know your relatives, but they are easy to recognize, they are people who frequently encounter problems and who create them.

As I mentioned in my first book, "*we have nothing for nothing*".

If you want to change your life, improve your daily life, you will have to take care of your friends, in short, change your circle, your socio-cultural environment, for two reasons:

- *Not to be considered among the wrong people.*

- *Learn from your new circle.*

Make new acquaintances, learn a little more about them, be passionate and, above all, read a lot! It can not hurt you, and a minimum of culture is required.

This is the price to pay to succeed, to get rid of one's own environment and to frequent another better adapted to what one wants to become, the mechanism must be done not brutally, like petting a cat in the direction of the hair, this tender animal will trust you and accept your attentions. On the other hand, if your hand is too heavy, be careful with scratches, he will suspect you.

There is no difference in terms of the environment between being without technology or telephone in a desert island and getting rich, these two situations are alien to your environment of life, metro, work and sleep (otherwise, it depends on you and it is not my business!), whose operation you know by heart.

You will have to learn these sociocultural codes of rich people, try to immerse yourself in this environment by reading, going to the restaurant and in the organized evenings, to immerse yourself in this silent atmosphere.

Preferably, first of all, get some information! This will prevent you from being seen as *Mr. Bean* eating lobster, or as a person who thinks you are at a "*Paulette's*" roadside bar, there is no roast beef with shallot sauce, but more refined dishes, behavior plays a role very important in making you accepted in this world.

In a second step, you will need some knowledge of wealth management, here too, there is no shortage of books on the subject! you will get new information, and unconsciously, without necessarily remembering everything the first time, this will be a first approach.

To add an element to this brief passage, during your conversations, do not talk too much, but let your interlocutor talk, a proportion of 20% of words for 80% of the information collected, avoid positioning yourself as an expert, without a doubt you will I would lift The individual in front of you has studied, has a greater knowledge than you, is professional, so the dialogue of your interlocutor must shake it.

You will get a gold mine from him, he will

thank you if you listen to him if he is curious, do not skimp on the questions, go ahead! Go from the selfish to the altruistic, you will feel through yourself, you will sweat sympathy, and your interlocutor will feel that we are interested in him, and he will become more and more sure of himself.

Ask questions by not letting your ignorance manifest, for example, in a painting exhibition, appear intrigued by a Modigliani painting (it does not matter who you do not know), "pretend" to your next-door neighbor by saying things like "*interesting*"," *It's strange! "What do you think of this painting?* "(to collect information).

As you do this, you will acquire a little more experience, not necessarily studying fine arts, but gleaning.

The direction to take in life

Your thoughts are personal to you, and no one can influence what you really want, you are free to express your political opinions, about society, about your professional options. Throughout your life, you will meet people who want to change your course, but in reality, they would not like to see you succeed, they are influential people.

What you really want must come from your feelings, it is your heart that must speak and your mind to think.

Not everyone thinks like you, you have to to deal with the idea, and fortunately there are different opinions, because they open the debate.

So, get the great Lulu or the Nelly Olson out of your memory, they have only been a part of your life, but they do not make your life, and your encounter with this type of people should be a reinforcement and not a brake, the Past experiences should strengthen you and that is how you should see things.

So that you have an idea of what you should do, listen to his heart. If you are passionate about one or more trades, it is in these areas where you should go. Finding what gives your emotions more intensity is what gives an exciting side to your existence.

Do not let fear dominate your life, fight it, ignore the mockery, sometimes it's enough to say to yourself: "*Oh, what the hell, I'm going to go for it!*" And from that moment, give yourself the means ! In the age of Internet and other media, you have a large number of tools at your disposal that can be used.

When you do not dare, it's mostly because you do not have the will, but is it because you do not have the confidence to do it because you do not have enough information?

"How can this be achieved?" *"Am I made for this job? "* *" Where do I go? "* These are some of the questions that run through your mind as you circle around without knowing what to do.

To be successful and be a better version of yourself, you will have to overcome your fears and doubts, not stop being defeatist and be so *"curious about everything"*.

Open the books, push the doors of the training organizations, even if your subconscious mind whispers to not try, listen to your heart and let your emotions speak. Fear is what prevents you from reaching your dreams, breaking that barrier.

The more you feel this feeling of fear and external doubt in what you are passionate about internally, the closer you will be to the goal.

When you know exactly what you want, do not deviate from the path your heart has dictated to you, this is your final goal in life, nothing will be simple, but you will have to work hard to achieve it, and nobody but you can influence it.

You are not incapable or useless, but you lack training.

The only person responsible for your life is you. In fact, not always, when we were children, adults taught us fields of values, we all evolved in our social environment, and we knew that the information was related to it.

It is never too late to take charge of your life, life is a succession of possibilities, it is up to us to take advantage of them, either to follow the beliefs that they have taught us, or to demonstrate the opposite of everything you have been taught, and that those who have criticized you are wrong, and it is on this basis that we must work on your mind, create new ideas that obscure the ideas received.

From now on, train yourself to think differently. You are not incapable, but it is true that you lack information and that you have to look for it.

The more you know, the more ignorant will seem to you all those who despise you. Of course, they will continue to criticize you, but as you think about it, they will have the shock of their lives when they discover at what level you are in relation to them, and they will begin to shut you up, because deep down, there are many people happy with our misfortune, which allows them to Establish your ego so that you can exist.

The restrictions of our subconscious mind

They are specific to the individual and can be summarized in an uncultured mind, is limited by lack of habit, when you read a book for example, you will find this boring or boring either because the challenge of reading more than 200 pages seems insurmountable, or because you do not understand a word feature of what is said in it, without knowing any of the barbarian terms used by the author.

Our brains, like our muscles, need training and nutrients to function.

If I make a comparison between lifting weights of 25 kg and growing, in both cases, training is needed.

Without this, if your goal is to be able to do about 20 movements lifting heavier weights than your brain tells you (of course, one day you can do it, but not from the beginning), you will "*paralyze*", the more effort you make, and More insurmountable will seem, because you want everything and immediately, that is, for many weightlifters or relatively, those who are successful, have a very good way to achieve their goals through tools called "patience" and "*perseverance*".

To do this, you need to create a schedule in your mind, to tell yourself that every day you do such exercises, in my case for example, I spend at least one hour a day reading, and another time writing, and depending on the enthusiasm, I can do a little more.

Keep in mind your goals, you have to row a little to get to the promised land, the ship will not advance alone, and will divert you to another destination that you really do not want to go to.

Every day, make small efforts, integrate them into your habits, and the easier it seems, and the more you progress to the next level thanks to the habit generated, you will reap the benefits of your efforts.

At one point in my life, I was fascinated by a writer, J.R.R. TOLKIEN, whom you probably know from writing the Lord of the Rings trilogy.

I discovered this author thanks to my cousin who lent me one of his books called "*Bilbo the Hobbit*". By the way, I recommend that you read it, you will discover the meaning of having a "*real treasure*".

Believe me or not, inside you there is a great

gold mine that only needs to be exploited, only that, at some point in your life, you have stopped digging many galleries that lead to real treasures. You were missing the tools, shovels, picks, etc ...

These tools, you get them through the information that gives you everything you need to dig deeper and deeper into your mind, revealing beautiful deposits.

To return to the trilogy of Lord of the Rings, do not embark on the adventure of reading the whole trilogy, do not put yourself in the position of having this goal in mind, suddenly you will be discouraged, I recommend you start small, with books that only have 150 or 200 pages. By the way, a book like "*The secret door to success*" by *Florence Schoven* Shin has only 140 pages and is easy to read.

A book is sacred, it is not bought in fashion,or for to complete the library, maybe the spiders who weave their webs on it will read it, you get it because you really care about the author, because you are interested in history and want to discover it, or because you look for information. In addition, a writer, through his writings, has a message to convey, a story to tell that he does not want to see

The more your brain is trained to accept information, and the more your thirst for knowledge grows, some even become addicted.

Clear your mind

To get rid of your old life and be the person you always wanted to be, you need to clear your mind, for this you will have to sit on a chair or lie down on the bed, and then do not think about anything.

You have to practice clearing your mind every day, or if you can not, as regularly as possible, stop thinking about the painful events of the day, the bad news, an irritable boss, the car that breaks down .... Everyone.........

To help you do this, set a specific point in the room, for example, a trinket, the phone or a can on the table. Focus only on this object.

Start enjoying this little moment of calm, and focus on your goal, although for the moment it may be in the shape of a can or trinket.

Take the wheat out of the straw

In all the situations of our existence, we all have the good and the bad, a part of painful events hides something better for us, we simply detect it.

When my father died in 2011, I thought that the world was collapsing around me, so stunned by this painful event that it was impossible for me to think correctly, I was lost. It was one of my pillars that had just collapsed. It was urgent that I recover and not let the situation dominate me, it is at one of these specific moments when we learn to take responsibility and to be mentally stronger, if it were not for those who do not have the ability to recover as quickly as possible.

We are all pillars in life, we are always useful to humanity when we decide not to surrender, and it is from this moment that we discover our inner strength. For that, what can I offer you to become a mentally stronger person?

Almost everything is said in this book, but I would like to focus on some important points, such as the real conditioning of the subconscious mind through a neuroassociated connection.

This method consists of taking the good out of all the bad moments of your existence, I give you an example, if you are reading my book, it is that you are still alive and that there is still that little inner voice that pushes you to act, on the other hand , your subconscious blocks you saying "I can not!"

First of all, when you think about your past life, at all the painful moments, the great Lulu that harassed you in the school yard, you tell yourself that it made you mentally stronger.

Generally, those individuals who terrified you when you were younger are almost close to what we might call "*narcissistic perverts*".

They need to base their domination on someone weaker for their personal safety, towards their comrades to be part of the gang, but without them, it would be nothing. Originally they are weak people who do not want to show anything, and the fact of dominating you as a child gave them a feeling of superiority, made it stronger.

These people, in this case, transfer their weaknesses to another person, they are never responsible and if they do not change course, they never will be.

What it means to be responsible in this sense, means "*to assume*", "to recognize one's mistakes", the latter being a quality called "*noble*", what is even better is the possibility of self-correction, of reasoning. Then, tell yourself that you are and you will always be stronger than all those who have despised you.

Never fall into the trap of criticism (tares) and take it constructively (good grain), because judgment and criticism can only go in two directions if you meditate on what I teach you, self-correction and substitution, that is, if you take note of the errors and relativize everything that is said to you, and who tells you, and in any case, remember this:

"*YOU KNOW YOUR OWN VALUE*"

Relativize each event in a positive way, if you had not known "*the great Lulu*" in your life, you would be stronger today.

The exterior reflects the interior

It may seem surprising to you what I am saying here, if you have not yet assimilated the power of conscious and unconscious self-suggestion. I will try to be as explicit as possible, because I really want you to be successful in your life, that is the mission of this book, to give you the keys to a better life.

The world that you build in your imagination must "*sweat*" outward, that is, put your mind in line with everything that happens around you.

In short, imagine that you have a bank account that is often overdrawn, and that your month ends are difficult, the reminder letters remind you constantly, and your subconscious is always in phase with this situation, accustomed to these circumstances, It will be a reason, and it will be difficult for you to be connected to positive circumstances. Conscious and unconscious autosuggestion will not be enough.

You idealize your life, but your perception and feelings towards the outside world are not connected.

So when you imagine yourself being rich and prosperous, this is not the case in the real world.

Why does not the materialization of your wishes work?

Because you are simply not in tune with the outside world, you perceive and feel the present moment, there is a gap between the inner being, convinced that you will not succeed, because you have forged a boring reality, do not have the intimate conviction that the Things will change despite your ideas and positive suggestions.

The easiest way would be to let it go, you can not stop things from happening, these events are really present in your life.

On the other hand, from now on, impacts can be cushioned, as they do not try to provoke complex events.

Ask yourself how you can improve this situation by recording the causes of your problems step by step on a piece of paper. Do you smoke or drink? Do you have a first job that gives you a decent income? Determine what you earn and what you spend, and identify areas for improvement! All this to bring the conscious and the unconscious closer, what you imagine must come from outside, everything must be felt outside, around you. For a moment, stop for a moment and ask yourself, "What am I doing? »On the one hand, there is the real world with its limitations and problems that need to be improved, and on the other hand, there is the imagination where the predominant feeling is uncertainty.

What direction should we take to recover a serene mood? Start sorting your relationships and stop dating people who really do not want to get away with it or who despise you. Go to places where you can meet people, such as libraries or associations. Pay off your debts starting with the smallest ones, even if you have bigger claim letters, anyway, you will not have the money to settle them all, so to alleviate your problems, start with the smallest ones, which will leave room in your mind to find solutions for the rest.

Stop spending unnecessarily, it is part of bad habits, even for small amounts, because it gives the feeling of not spending much, while small accumulated amounts make it big. As a result, your mood will no longer be under the sword of Damocles of need, you will have enough to live, you must reach "*sufficiency*", that feeling where you do not need anything.

The notions of gains and losses

There are two notions, lack and gain, and success or failure depends on how you see them.

Speaking in terms of "*deprivation*", "*remaining sum*" or even "*economy*" sweats the "lack", you do not have enough ..... You do not have enough .... It's very little ....., All these phrases are a reflection of your thoughts, it is your reality.

It is rare to hear someone say: "*Great, I have in my possession the sum of 1 €, it's extraordinary.*" (by not putting the "*yet*"), most of the time you hear "*I only have 1 € left*". Do you start to see the difference?

It has already happened to you to see 1 cent on the ground, the reflection for some is to collect this coin, for others, it is to leave it on the ground, because the sum seems ridiculous, and yet .... By not accepting it , you turn your back on money, because you consider that it does not benefit you, while others, considering it as a profit (without looking at the small amount), will repeat this situation when you do not think about it, because many say *"this is the beginning of Wealth* ", in effect, but affirm that it remains in the field of" lack "(You need ..... you hope ...).

As I have mentioned, your inner thoughts must "*sweat*" outward, that is, you linearize your perception that tends to reality, your subconscious needs to consider something as "*true*", because what you are experiencing is only the accumulation of what you have affirmed in your whole life, you must for this transform the notion of lack by the notion of profit, if your mind is oriented towards it, it will attract towards you everything you desire. If you make the firm decision to do this, with the force of habit, your subconscious will get used to saving, but in spite of everything, it will be oriented towards the notion of retirement if you look too closely at your savings.

Inside you, he will whisper to you: "*I can not spend this amount, because I am limited financially*". For this to really work, and for you to reap all the benefits, far beyond your expectations, your mind must look at the efforts made and not the sacrifices made to achieve it. That is, consider what you have left as a profit that you can accumulate (this redirects the subconscious towards the notion of abundance), your perception should be the following, if you earn for example 1200 € net per month (French reference salary), if you opt for the automatic deduction and if you have 50 € or 100 € left at the end of the month, when you think "*remain-*

ing sum", it will influence your mind towards the lack.

I have read many books on personal development, but what I find very unfortunate is that most of these books do not explain it clearly. When you have a TV, it's a profit, a roof over your head, it's a gain, the same when you have a job (no matter what it is), if you can concentrate on the content and not on the form, you will understand that you are already very rich and you win every time you get something out of life.

I was talking about the laws of the subconscious, and the most important of these is the law of balance. The interior must "*sweat*" outward, now try to imagine having the possibility to see yourself and be all that symbolizes the universe, the environment in which you live and the people you know! Taking your place, in what mood would you be if, for example, and taking the role of the universe, you gave life, the possibility of interacting, of seeing the world around you, of touching, of listening, and that in return, what you see (yourself), despite everything you offer, will be unsatisfied? The one in front of you has got everything from you (as a universe), but in return, it is only resentment, envy and selfishness, because it gives nothing, does not give thanks and does not make any small gesture in this direction, for example, contributing to improve the world.

The practicing Catholics, at the beginning of each meal, give the blessings, that is, they say a prayer to thank the Lord for the food they are going to eat, it has a symbolic meaning, because they are grateful to have bread on the table and wine for to drink.

Enjoy and be proud of what you have! And thank the universe for what it offers, even if the current situation saddens you, while you are in a state of bitterness, to affirm that you have a life of misery, you will only obtain a life of misery from the universe.

This way of reacting comes from your subconscious, when you were a child, and your parents took you to the supermarket, some of you were capricious, especially when passing through the candy section, claiming and making a scene in front of the other customers, imagine the heads of your father and your mother, already warmed by your behavior.

This same phenomenon also happened during the Christmas holidays, if you remember well, your family gave you gifts when you were very young, although you were not wise, so, having become accustomed to being given toys at that time, over the years, you understood less and less why they gave you less and less, which indirectly created the sense of lack. This is what happens with children who are too spoiled, accustomed to receiving everything at a very early age, they end up becoming individuals who depend on others and who, above all, are mostly engaged in cheating their parents.

Envy someone for what they have is synonymous with lack, because you want what you have besides you, be it a nice car or a nice villa with a pool, you will not get anything from all this because indirectly, you punish yourself, because your subconscious mind is oriented towards need, what you do not have, what puts you in a position of poverty and with this state of mind, your feelings will be similar to those of a beggar, sitting on the ground looking at the people who have the the smallest piece to provide it.

You ask and wait for everything to happen to you if you already enjoy what you have. Most people spend their lives ruminating about their difficult situation, read my book, and without changing their mood, I would say that everything that is pointed out in this book is pure nonsense, whereas from my point of view, Like so many others who have succeeded, we are still true and everything is in the process of being realized.

Recently, I attended a congress for a bar turning company celebrating its 40th anniversary. During his speech, the group's president made the story of his rapid progress.

At the beginning of the adventure that this company was going to live, there was only one workshop in a garage and only the founder of what would become a giant of the metallurgical industry in *Haute-Savoie*.

This man, alone in his garage, was the father of the man who would later become president of the group, was a determined, rigorous person, and made quality his goal, which allowed him to be recognized for his know-how and win new customers .

Soon after, this small workshop could no longer meet a large demand, so it took an employee and, shortly after, bought a larger workshop. Over time, thanks to his tenacity, and being a great worker, was a company that grew a little more, and every time he had to meet the expectations of an expanding clientele, he took over new facilities, new machines and new employees.

The president of this group related his beginnings, first as an employee, to take care of one of his father's workshops, taking as a model his rigor and determination that made him progress.

Throughout his speech, I saw a man with the same enthusiasm, always advancing, showing us his vision of the company, his words were not aimed at lack, but progress, proud of the progress made, his goal was excellence, I had the impression of attending a seminar on personal development and the group president seemed to speak like a coach.

Reach new markets, and obtain a global influence, that's what the group has become, an international brand with companies in the United States, Poland or Switzerland among others, imagine the path taken from almost nothing, in the speech, did not make reference to the lack, everything was focused on profit, success and progress. This is the perspective you must have, always strive for excellence and be proud of what you have. Without claiming anything from life, try to convince yourself that you can always do better.

Free your mind from your problems

If you are drowning in difficulties, do not worry and try to analyze the situations in a rational way. As mentioned above, a weightlifter never starts with heavier weights, you will not get anywhere thinking that this is impossible, first, analyze why it seems insurmountable, starting with the base. Remove some weights from your weights, represent your problems and start to solve them starting with the smallest of them, with the training, the impossible will be possible, from 5 kg, you will pass to 10 kg, this step will be possible for you.

By being patient, after a month, two months and so on, your body will gradually get used to it.

If you start with 5 kg problems, your mind will adapt if you give it the vitamins it needs in the form of information, your brain feeds on it through reading and documentation.

Therefore, they have weapons to solve very small difficulties, which will become less restrictive for their mind, will be freed from certain burdens, leaving more space to solve larger problems.

It's simple, start with the smallest problems and finish with the biggest ones to solve.

Do not give up to the sound of sirens.

It is the secret to a better life, to know what is really important to you and what is not. In the following pages, I will earn you a lot of money (this will bring the price of this book, which is the best investment of your life)

Do the accounts and see what you have left at the end of the month, why are you often or always in the red? Earning money does not necessarily mean receiving money from a third party, but preserving your capital. When you buy, you see products on the shelves you want, a touchpad, a smartphone, a video game console, but you ask yourself this simple question for all these objects, "*do I really need them?*" If you already have a smartphone, why buy? one, the model is newer, the one you do not like anymore, or simply that it no longer works, in all these cases, act according to the pro rata, you have objects that work, then why change them?

Take stock of your priorities! At the beginning of the month, many people (not all of them) make the mistake of seeing the large amount of money that enters their bank account, no matter what comes out of it, so at the end of the month, the capital is somewhat limited , even null.

Set your budget according to who comes out, and not for what comes in, at the beginning of the month, deduces the priorities, ie rent, electricity, water, food, drink, etc ... You do not earn the full salary, because everything It leaves immediately to liquidate everything that is important, in reality, you only receive the rest of your income that constitutes your income. But you perceive this as a remnant, which is synonymous with lack, while you would have to think like this: "*I have this amount at my disposa*l".

What is most important to you? be at the forefront of technology to not appear as a "*has been*", or have a roof over your head and enough to meet your needs ... to spend or capitalize ... One thing is to want, and another the benefit .

During the week, I often went to the bakery after work (I worked at night) and I took a cake that cost around 1 €, which means that in a week I spent 5 € and in a month 20 €. This sum may seem ridiculous, but combined with others, it is possible to spend, in most cases, up to one hundred euros. Imagine that in a year, this represents around 1200 € (rounded).

If you go to the supermarket to get the best pastry brand, you can manage it for only 2 € or 3 € per week, that is, 8 € at the end of the month, and so on. Calculating your priorities first and making your team last a year or two, you could save money, and that's not all, that amount you saved, you can put it in a brochure of the carrier (check interest rates), and make money (if you put this in compound interest), I will conclude by telling you what my mother told me "*it is the small streams that make the great rivers*", remember!

CHAPTER 9: REPROGRAMMING TECHNIQUES

"Instinct needs to be trained by the method, but only instinct helps us to discover a method that is unique to us and thanks to which we can train our instinct."
(Jean Cocteau)

The subject was treated in my first book, only that you had to read it; if not, fortunately for you, I mention it again.

Take a paper and a pencil, draw two lines from top to bottom to separate the sheet in three. In the middle, you will notice all the events of your life that you will remember. The title of this column will be "*featured events*".

On your left, you will notice in the title "lack", why did you miss it? Did it come from you or your relatives, in your opinion?

On the right, the column will be called "the victory", what did you get? Thanks to whom? And your mood during this event.

Now, count the number of positive attributes and the number of negative attributes in each column. If there is more than one side or the other, it is the perception that you normally have of the world that surrounds you, it symbolizes your degree of difficulty nowadays.

For these same events, those that you have experienced as a lack, try to find an answer within yourself, why do you perceive these events negatively?

Reconsider your perception of these events and think about how the situation could have improved, do not blame the people who caused this event, it's about how you react, rethink positively, put things in perspective. Think of this as an advantage, for example , a job you could not do, maybe you were not prepared enough, or you were not done for work, or you were jealous of a classmate who was courting a girl you liked, maybe she was not made for you and You could do better.

When you search well, there is always a response from your subconscious that remains true, suffers your reality, you do not have the girl you liked, or the job you wanted, much less the amount you would have liked, because everything is geared towards " *lack*".

You are here, with me through my writings, very alive, you are in my company, right?

Think of everything that brought you to me (at least this book), what made you buy it? It is probably to find the answers you need, and you have already obtained a good part of them. The answers I try to give you to all the problems you have had in your life are in you, only that it is difficult to perceive them, because you are drowned in difficulties or you have not dared, too installed in your comfort zone, the girl you loved never It will have come to you, because there has not been any interaction with it, just as for the trade you expected, how would they have known of your existence?

It's not that different from showing up at a temporary employment agency or registering at a dating site, or opening an account on Facebook, "*at least they know you exist*".

The problem does not come from them, it comes from yourself, from the way you perceive the events, hence the interest to immerse yourself in your memories and take stock of everything that has brought you here.

But I will not let you sink, your life will take a new turn after reading this book, there is nothing magical about it, and I promised you a diagram that will follow this passage of this chapter, done with my little hands, is not it wonderful?

Now take another sheet of paper and start creating three columns again! One for "*lack*", another for "*significant events*" and the third for "*gain*".

Take your first page again, and look at the column on the left! Try to put an answer that symbolizes gains or profits on the second sheet! The girl you invited when you were young was not interested in you, and anyway, the relationship would have been complicated, having a different way of thinking, but it allowed you to meet a person with whom you feel good and who shares your life, you love your wife, but if you are single, you will know her without waiting for her, because waiting is synonymous with lack, I can recommend you, be well in your life, happy to have what you have, and if you are rich in what you have inside you, it will materialize outward. To do this, imagine your ideal woman and feel the love you have for this person, live in your mind in the present moment, and above all, save it for yourself, you have no hope and you enjoy, it is to appreciate every little moment with which, day after day, you will attract everything you want.

But nothing will happen by itself, you will have to interact with the outside world, make friends, make friends, put some energy into it, and perhaps one of these friends will introduce you to his sister, and above all, under no circumstances should you do it with a spirit of expectation. What appears inside will materialize outside, build your couple spirit, and it will come true, because the universe will re-balance events.

Going back to your sheet, where are you? Did you notice what I just told you? Dammit! Put your heart in it! Ahead! Ahead! Find out how negative events would have taken a positive turn, put it in perspective!

To summarize you or me, because you are probably in the interrogation, taking your two pages, renaming "*the lack*" by "*Follower*" and "*the gain*" by "*Leader*", you will understand in what position you are. The Follower follows the Leader, awaits instructions given to him, such as a student who expects the teacher to instruct him by giving him information that will be useful in life through the books, or as the sheep following the pastor, or the unemployed who expect to be offered work.

The Leader, on the other hand, does not expect

anything, or rather, gives time, energy, support, because he has a lot. If you watch the videos of *Franck Nicolas* or *Max Piccinini*, they also give to charity, they will not see them begging for their books, of course, they are forced to make themselves known through advertising, what is called "*interacting*" , the singer gives a message through a song, the politician leads the activists giving hope, express their ideas and make themselves known.

To succeed in life, it must come from a personal contribution! Stop being like the puppy that follows his master, be the "*Master*"! Give your time and energy, this is what the universe expects from you, your contribution has been made largely by putting them on this earth.

When I was in school, we had studied the weights, there was a scale called "*Roberval*" in the classroom, there were two trays, in one we placed weights of 20 g, 50 g and 100 g On the other hand, we had to determine the weight of an object It was a ballpoint pen, a rubber band or a tube of glue. If there were missing weights (the lack), the trays where the objects were placed remained at the bottom (where is your life), on the contrary, adding weights in the first table (the addition, the gain, the benefit), the second it has increased (it is your esteem, your thoughts and your life that take a better level).

So do not hesitate! Add some weight to your life and you will see that it will rise to a good level, and the more you wear it, the more it will rise.

Spirit oriented towards lack

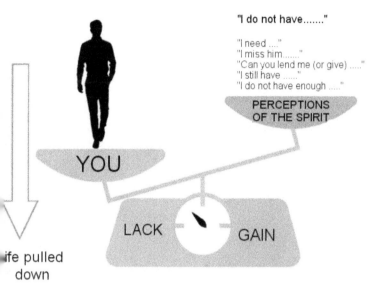

"I do not have......."

"I need ...."
"I miss him......."
"Can you lend me (or give) ....."
"I still have ....."
"I do not have enough ....."

PERCEPTIONS
OF THE SPIRIT

YOU

LACK   GAIN

ife pulled
down

Spirit oriented towards gain

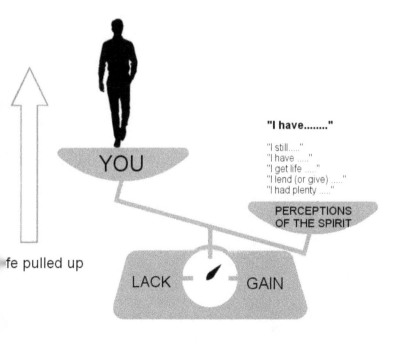

YOU

"I have........"

"I still....."
"I have ....."
"I get life ....."
"I lend (or give) ....."
"I had plenty ....."

PERCEPTIONS
OF THE SPIRIT

LACK   GAIN

fe pulled up

An effective resource

If I told you that there is a treatment that would encourage your subconscious to accept everything you ask, you would find it extraordinary, and yet, throughout this book, I have emphasized many points, including the phenomenon of subjective repetition. "*What the hell is that?*" Would you just tell me that insisting on an issue related to your personal life, be it health or finances, is also valid in other areas?

In therapeutic medicine, we call it "*conscious self-suggestion*" or "*Émile Coué method*", but as I mentioned, this technique only really works when we really believe in it. To do this, we must not only repeat the following formula: "*every day, in every way, every time I'm better*", accompanied by a sense of well-being.

If you do not know, then you can do what is called "*truncate*" or "*schinter*" or simply "*bridge*" between the formulation and a happy memory (we all have it, no matter how long it lasts).

Think of the feelings you experienced at your wedding, your first child, when you received a diploma or another, this happy memory resides somewhere in your consciousness, concentrate on it for a long time until it invades your whole being.

From this happy memory, he keeps only the emotions, then he formulates the phrase "*every day, from all points of view, I am getting better and better*". If you follow my recommendations, I can guarantee that it really works, not in a day, it would be too nice, but the results can already be felt after a few weeks, a few months, depending on the people, the degree of involvement and the level of difficulties solve.

The awakening of consciousness

For that, we'll do a little experiment. Take a book on a subject that seems painful to read. This can be in philosophy, mathematics, French or history. For those who want to do the most challenging exercise, take complicated topics such as accounting and legal issues. Read the chosen book at once, without trying to know the passages of memory, just read it.

You will have the impression that you are not learning anything, and yet your subconscious will function as a "*déjà vu*" system, unconsciously, you have retained information, even only 10%, which is not so bad.

The information will exist in your subconscious, but you will not know what to associate it with, you will have to wait for new information to create a correspondence with what you already know, a bridge will be created between the point of origin (your knowledge) and the new information, soon it will be more easy for your subconscious to process new data, as you read or document.

In the days, months or years to come, this information will remain engraved in a corner of your head. They will reappear when you need them, a kind of "*déjà vu*" effect, you will say to yourself *"I've seen this before somewhere!"* All our life, consciously or not, we continue to learn, our brain is a very large database, so we do not use much of the capabilities of this organ, it revolves around the maximum 30% of its capacities for a highly educated person, a average person only uses between 10 and 20%. And yet, billions of information circulate every second, it is the most sophisticated of all computers.

The technique of 1 cent coins

You are going to say: "*What else can a tech-*

nique like this bring to my life?" You think in such a way that you see how small and I would respond that even with 1 cent, you can do a lot, I'll show you.

For what I will show you, you will have to be conscientious, even very serious. This technique, incredible as it may seem, can save you a lot of money if you put your heart into it.

The purpose of this technique has two phases, the first is based on the concrete, you will see that what I propose is quite feasible, the second allows you to realign with the real, what the subconscious wants is that everything you think is authentic, true, achievable.

It will create a phenomenon, that of abundance, what you will do in the real world will also happen in your subconscious mind, it is one of the most important rules of the law of attraction, the exterior must also be felt inside, it must reflect a truth that your mind will assimilate, and the more you push up, and the more you are attracted in this direction by an invisible force, you will bathe in a magnetic aura that will attract to you all that you desire.

First, check your bank account and proceed as I said in the previous pages.

Solve your problems starting with the smallest, so that you are no longer in a situation that seems impossible to manage, and then gradually resolve the larger ones by negotiating friendly settlements with your creditors. In most cases, they will agree, subject to additional costs, but it is preferable to solve everything without waiting for major problems to arise.

Then, prepare a budget for the month, deducing from your salary all the basic expenses, that is, rent, electricity, etc ...

With the remaining amount, divide it by 4 weeks, then remove 25% of the weekly result, this will give you the maximum limit of expenses. And with the rest, although there are only a few €uros, leave them aside, it will be used for the 1 cent coin method.

Finally, I come to my technique, which has two objectives: to make you earn money and recondition your subconscious mind by the force of habit, this will be done naturally. For many of you, you will be surprised.

For this, you will need a large jar or box that you will place in a closed place, that is not directly exposed to the view, to avoid what could be called "*the torture of Tantalio*".

Start from this line that you read with only 1 cent. The bottle or box will appear empty at first, but if you are patient, you will reap the benefits of this effort.

The next day, deposit 1 cent + 1 cent, and the next day, add another 1 cent to your other 2 cents, and so on.

This method works in combination and it is not necessary to invest a lot of money in it at the beginning.

The ultimate goal is that just a few pennies, a coin is added into the pot or box at a time, and most extraordinary is that in fixing the limit of 1 €, ie, to give just one penny at a time to 0,99 €, first, it only takes 3 months and 9 days (the month rounded to 30 days), the total amount obtained will be 49.50 € .... Is not it amazing? Take the test with your calculator and imagine what you could earn in 6 months! A total of 161.90 € to reach the limit of 1.80 €.

This probably makes you aware of all the small expenses that you make during these 6 months and that do not exceed 2 € a day, it is the increase in added value that causes this phenomenon, and even more, for the bravest, try the same experience, but with 0.10 € per day, the sum (multiplied by 10) accumulated would represent a total of 1,619 € for 18 € in 6 months (if possible!).

Still do not believe me? 1 € per day, in a period of one month, already represents 30 € and in 6 months, 180 €. If you start this technique now, your subconscious mind will not accept it at first, but with the force of habit, will become routine to do it, so you have to think about yourself, take control of yourself, and you will become in something natural.

Make your money work

Many will say that I'm away from my initial theme, while it is not, it is part of the reacondition the subconscious mind and make it assimilate the concepts of saving, which will radically change your life, and if you do thoroughly, so will do without even thinking, your subconscious mind will also make your money work, because he will think otherwise. With the money you have saved, you can expect at least 50 € per month, which I advise you to gradually invest in a savings account, for a year, you will have acquired 600 € in addition to the interest rates. This will allow you to go up with the accumulation of coins 0.01 €, I advise you to save money because the method can have its limits if you do not follow these recommendations to the letter, especially if you have to withdraw sums of up to 10 € per day, you will have to resort to your savings.

I assure you that I go out for 10 € a day, although it may seem incredible, and you think I've fallen head over heels, it's very feasible, but it will not take you more than three years to get there. By booking your 50 € per month, ensures the continuity of the process to have a part of their capital. After three years, you will see your capital increase, abundance impregnate your subconscious, what happens inside you resonate with the outside world, which will have the effect of having the winning spirit, other changes will occur in your life if you reconsideras everything that you have had or possess since your childhood, you transform your weaknesses into strengths.

Imagine everything you can acquire, far beyond the announced 1939 €, will exceed all your expectations. Because everything will be attracted to you like a magnet.

The conscious suggestion

As I mentioned, there is a method that allows us to see things in the right light. This is the method of Émile Coué, which can be summarized in a score of reformulations, to convince itself that events and health are in the right place, only works if we are intimately convinced of their effectiveness and, above all, conscious autosuggestion it must be accompanied by emotions, and an inner well-being linked to the formulation must be felt. I modified it a little to give more strength to its effectiveness. Instead of using "*every day, every point of view, I'm getting better and better!*", if not rather "*every day, every point of view, I feel like I'm getting better and better!*"

Use this and try to feel a sense of well-being! If you have difficulty doing this, think of something nice that gives you pleasure, relax and get your problems out of your head. Try to separate the event from the emotion and make a transposition, that is, separate the memory from the experienced feeling.

A paperclip against a house

I remember a story that started very precisely on July 12, 2005 and ended a year later, on July 12, 2006, and I ask you now: is it possible to have a house in exchange for a paper clip?

Naturally and with a logical mind, no, because you think in terms of money, while the one that is at the origin of this story is called *Kyle M* has not paid a single penny.

As it did? It all started with a bet he made on himself when he saw a paper clip on his desk, that of acquiring a house from this small object with no apparent value, but that would allow him to realize his dream.

He puts his small paperclip in line at a barter site, and in return receives a fish-shaped pen, which will be exchanged for a knob, this will be given by a barbecue, and then gradually exchanges an electric generator, a beer pump, a snowmobile, a van, a record company to record a demo, a year of free rental in Phoenix, and over time, social networks, then the media are interested in him, and so, his bet continues, his free rental in Phoenix is punctured for an afternoon with *Alice Cooper*, who exchanges for a simple snowball.

Internet users who followed the case very closely found this choice quite regressive, while it was strategic, because they did not know that *Corbine Bersen* was a great collector of snowballs, and they offered her a role in her next film, to finish, and she arrived In early July

2006, he changed his small role in a movie to a house. All this in a year has been a succession of events that have led him to his final goal.

He did not say to himself, as many would say: "It's absurd", so, unlike this man, many do not try, or when they try, they give up on the road, but who made this bet is He clung to the end, set a final goal without really wondering how he would get there and if he would get there. Each object that has more and more value, his subconscious was always pulled up, goal after goal, created the phenomenon of attractiveness, external events changed around him, because he believed strongly in him. It has attracted Internet users, media and personalities throughout its history, which at first was not taken seriously, but over time, people have been convinced.

I wanted to show with this bet that people give too much importance to material value when it is enough to think about the subjective and emotional value, the test is done with the snowball exchanged with *Corbin Bernsen*.

Kyle MacDonald also appears in the Guinness Book of Records in the "Most Successful Internet Exchanges" category.

Neuroassociation and neuro-substitution

You are presented with an object and a signal is transmitted to your subconscious. Seek to associate with him, be it good or bad. For example, for a smoker, cigarettes will be synonymous with pleasure, because they give him his daily dose of nicotine.

For a non-smoker, this refers to health problems that can lead to death. I am not saying that a smoker does not think about it, but the desire to have a daily dose dominates the thought of the problems that may result.

Only when they arrive they realize that smoking is harmful, but it is too late. Your subconscious is working on priorities. The same is true for an alcoholic or a Facebook addict, they are addicted people. The song of the sirens is stronger than their will, always the subconscious mind that allows the object of their addiction to dominate. To compensate for the neuroassociation of dominant pleasure, there is a method that I have tried myself, that of substitution. It means *"finding another dominant pleasure"*. I remember when I was younger, I went out to nightclubs with my friends, I drank a lot of alcohol at that time in my life, but I also understood that I was losing all my clarity and risking a lot when getting my license.

So, I really do not remember in what context, I started drinking a lot of coffee (that's not good too, I know!), But this dose of caffeine was more essential to me than alcohol, I just had to replace one drink with another . The method used was to replace neuro-addiction with neuro-substitution by telling myself that coffee was more essential to me than alcohol, and since then, I no longer drink a drop of it outside events like Christmas and the Birthdays . All I can tell you is that it really works! Try it and you will see! If you use all your inner strength and put enthusiasm, a good dose of conviction and will be fine!

The echo of your subconscious mind

Now, I am going to suggest an exercise to recover the self-confidence that works in the visual, in the touch, in the verbal and in the subconscious, all at the same time. It consists in associating a single thing or event with all your senses. If you have no references, go to a luxury restaurant or hotel, preferably put on a suit that matches the decoration, and this will prevent the receptionist from asking you what you are doing here. In that case, tell him you're waiting for someone. Nothing could be easier.

Then, locate the places well, make the emptiness of your current life and in yourself, suppose that you have always known luxury, that the place is part of your habits, feel every sound, every movement of the crowd, absorbs all that surrounds you, this will serve as the basis for the rest of the experience.

Once the information is collected, you go home and lie down in your bed. Think about the situation you experienced. Do not do this with your current problems in mind, as I have already mentioned, the subconscious mind is based only on the real world, its emotions should not be oriented in any way towards envy and need, relive the scene as if it were really a customer of this restaurant yourself, and in no way associate all this with the money you spend or the loss, but rather with the benefit and pleasure that you bring to the menu.

If you have observed all the dishes that the clients of the luxury restaurant ate, you will have to associate them with your own senses, as if you had ordered the same dishes. Imagine the taste of meat, vegetables, wine, atmosphere and sounds. The scene repeats itself in your head. In this place, you meet people you know (always in your imagination), they are well-known people, they ask you for recommendations on the dishes before you sit down at your table. They talk to you about things and others, the food goes well, your guests are happy to be with you, and when you pay the bill, you tell your guests: *"Leave it for me"*, you have the means because you have an inexhaustible supply , *"you win"* the sympathy of the people around you, *"you win"* a beautiful evening, and *"win"* in all areas. Then, as you imagine this scene, repeat this orally, *"I am here now, this is the life I must have"*, then do the same in your mind, impregnate this phrase by repeating it mentally, cross the oral and the mental.

Meditate on this for at least one hour during the day, then, during your night's sleep, build the life you want to have, then you have all the elements to make it up. Having a great cultural capacity, I invite you to look for information, to be curious about everything that life has to teach you, to take out only the positive of all situations and the positive will come to you.

It is about reconsidering your whole existence, such is the purpose of this book, you are alive, in full health, you have at your disposal all the riches of this world, the power to extract from this inexhaustible reserve that are culture, abundant air that you breathe, what you already possess in you that has been "*won*", you are much richer than you think and you have much more to bring to the world around you, but in any case, it is still authentic, meditate on the latter words!

CONCLUSION

We are nearing the end of this book, hoping that it has been useful to you and that you have provided some answers to all the questions you asked yourself. Now you have many tools at your disposal to reprogram your subconscious mind and get a better life from it.

This will require a constant personal investment, especially in these last lines, if I have something to say to you, *"do not give up!"* The reward is often a great effort, you will thank you later, for my part, I only highlight what is already in you, I have already mentioned in my first book entitled *"Guaranteed Success"*, the advice I give in each of my books should follow you throughout your life, remember everything that has been listed.

Always concentrate on your goals, do not exaggerate, have confidence and gradually go, you will gain confidence, and this will help you to progress towards the final goal, success.

To know if there will be a follow-up of my two books, I do not know, time will tell me, and I do not have the habit of making promises that I can not keep, you'll see for yourself. In the meantime, whatever happens, I wish you every success in everything you do.

One last thing......

"*Always keep your mind above the line!*"

Friendly yours

Yoann MERITZA

READING SUGGESTIONS

BOD EDITIONS

- GUARANTEED SUCCESS
Yoann MERITZA

UN MONDE DIFFERENT

- RÉUSSITE MAXIMUM
Max PICCININI

- CONFIANCE ILLIMITÉE
Franck NICOLAS

- THE LAW OF ATTRACTION
Michael J. LOSIER

BELIVEAU EDITIONS

- 7 ESSENTIAL INGREDIENTS TO DOMI-
NATE THE LAW OF ATTRACTION
*Jack CANFIELD - Mark Victor HANSEN -
Jeanna GABELLINI - Eva GREGORY*

MARABOUT POCHE

- THE COUÉ METHOD
Emile COUE

- THE POWER OF POSITIVE THINKING
Norman Vincent PEAL

J'AI LU

- THE SECRET CODE OF YOUR DESTINY
James HILMAN

- MEET YOUR DESTINY
Wayne W. DYER

- WHEN YOU WANT, YOU CAN!
Normann Vincent PEAL

- HOW TO MAKE YOUR LIFE SUCCESS-
FUL?
Dr Josephe MURPHY

- HOW TO USE THE POWER OF YOUR
SUBCONSCIOUS MIND?
Dr Joseph MURPHY

- THE POWER OF WILL
Paul-Clément JAGOT

- THE GAME OF LIFE
Florence Scovel SHINN

- YOUR WORD IS A MAGICAL WAND
Florence Scovel SHINN

- THINK IT AND GET RICH
Napoleon HILL

- THE SECRETS OF COMMUNICATION
Richard BANDLER & John GRINDER

- BECOME A MENTALIST
Bastien BRICOUT

LIVRE DE POCHE

- HOW TO MAKE FRIENDS
Dale CARNEGIE

- HOW TO SPEAK IN PUBLIC
Dale CARNEGIE

ASKA EDITIONS

- MORE CLEVER THAN THE DEVIL
Napoleon HILL

ADA EDITIONS

- THE SECRETS OF SUCCESS
Sandra Anne TAYLOR

BUSSIERE EDITIONS

- THE DOOR SECRET TO SUCCESS
Florence Scovel SHINN

CPSIA information can be obtained
at www.ICGtesting.com
Printed in the USA
LVHW050436300920
667478LV00006B/843

9 782322 152063